The Pro ♥ Child Way

Parenting with an Ex

*Lucky for your child, it only takes **you** to make a significant impact on the divorced-parenting tone.*

Library of Congress Control Number: 2009934661
ISBN: 978-0-9820834-3-7

THE PRO♥CHILD WAY is a service mark of Ellen Kellner.

Published by UnTapped Talent LLC
Hershey, PA 17033-0396
www.UnT2.com

Cover illustration by Rachel Dunham; heart center by Patti Van Brederode
Printed in the United States of America.

to
Sarah and Acadia

You're so important to me
that my love for you
forced me to figure it out and keep doing it.

I plead on bended knees for them.
They will suffer and when they do
we will be the ones who are guilty
for not having done all in our power
to protect and love them.
— Mother Theresa

BEFORE GETTING STARTED

LETTER TO THE READER

SECTION 1: Here and There

SECTION 2: Parents Together

SECTION 3: Communication

Communicating with Your Child and Your Ex 61

SECTION 4: The Money Issue

Don't Let Money Become the Issue, The Issue
Is Raising Your Child 77

SECTION 5: Beyond the Three of You

Extended Families... 99

SECTION 6: Behavior Issues

Dealing with Discipline and Behavior 115

BEFORE GETTING STARTED
The Author's Assumptions

I write this book as a mother who has an ex and a daughter. If you are a father with an ex, read "Dad" where you see "Mom." If you have a son, read "he" instead of "she." The advice is universal, regardless of the pronouns.

I write this book assuming that you are a good parent. Like me, you wake up in the morning thinking how you and your child can have a good day. Like me, you lie in bed at night thinking of the choices you made that day as a parent, wondering if you could have done better. You are the type of good parent that would pick up a book on divorced-parenting and read it.

I write this book assuming that your ex is a good parent. Sure the two of you may have been awful as husband and wife, but as a parent, your ex was fine. Might you have some complaints about his parenting skills? Probably. But if he loves his child and if he is concerned about her well-being, then he classifies as a good parent. Would he pick up a book on divorced-parenting and read it? Probably not. Lucky for your child, it only takes **you** to make a significant difference on the divorced-parenting tone.

I'm not a lawyer. I'm not a psychologist. I'm a mom who was stressed, exhausted, and disappointed as I frantically looked for a book to help me raise my child through divorce. This is my response to not finding what I was looking for. My insights and advice are only based on my own experience and bolstered by my spiritual convictions. I feel that when love for your child is the motivator, you can never go wrong.

Now let's get started!

♡ *Lucky for your child, it only takes **you** to make a significant difference on the divorced-parenting tone.*

LETTER TO THE READER
If I Can Do It, So Can You!

This book on pro-child parenting after divorce isn't a collection of research, surveys, or field studies. This is my life. These are my children's lives – both my older child with her dad and my younger child with her dad. Two children. Two exes. The phrase, "She knows every trick in the book," doesn't refer to a dog. It refers to me. I know "tricks" number 1 through 46. I've "been there, done that" twice with all 46 situations. I've been tempted by the old way of divorced-parenting. And at times, to satisfy my own ego, I've slid down that nasty old path – only to find my child's needs laying in the proverbial trash can along with my heart.

My children are so important to me. I want them to grow up in a world seeing others' needs, not wrapped up in their own needs. I want them to experience joy, love, compassion, and wonder. I realized quickly that in order to instill that in them, I had to be a good parent. Which means I have to be an excellent, thinking, and full-of-conviction divorced parent.

I am raising my daughters as a parent should. The fact that their other parent is my ex plays very little in the final choices that I make regarding their upbringing, even though it is considered normal to travel a different divorced-parenting path. It seems that society encourages spiteful, ego-filled divorced-parenting. It's all too easy to blindly follow this old way of divorced-parenting. Instead, I'm actively choosing a new way of thinking. A thinking that listens more to my heart than to the chatter in my mind.

This is why I wrote a book. I challenge society's old ways that are so detrimental to children of divorce. I realize that when you take time to be still and consider your child, you'll remember that good parenting skills are absolute and not corrupted by marital status. A child needs love, time, structure, consideration, respect, and discipline. A good parent strives to provide these things and more.

My children are so important to me. I want them to grow up in a world seeing others' needs, not wrapped up in their own needs. I want them to experience joy, love, compassion, and wonder.

The Pro♡Child Way: Parenting with an Ex is based on the truth that I can only change my divorced-parenting behavior by first recognizing where I am at. If I am angry, spiteful, resentful, or sorrowful towards my ex, I will parent that way until I recognize that that is where I am. My children feel where I am. Once I get real with where I am, I'm amazed at how easily the Pro♡Child Way follows.

Being still is very powerful. Within the stillness, I can hear love speak. I can feel what other divorced-parenting choices I can make that would nurture my children. Simply by recognizing my ego-based reaction and choosing another way, my children are shielded from my attitude and nurtured in the Pro♡Child Way. I am a parent. A parent who handles divorced situations. And in this mindful world of parenting with an ex, I am choosing the Pro♡Child Way.

I'm not special. I didn't attend years of classes on child psychology, parenting, or conflict resolution. I am simply a mom who made a choice to not use the old way of divorced-parenting as my way. I want my children to grow up knowing that they are loved very much. Pro♡Child parenting is the result, and every day I continue to make that choice. If I can do it, so can you …
If I can do it, YOU CAN TOO!

— Ellen

WORDS OF ENCOURAGEMENT
You can set the tone, with or without your ex's help.

Talk about fighting a battle on your own! When you choose to parent the Pro♡Child Way, it may seem at times – or all the time – that you are indeed fighting a battle on your own. When your child's well-being is at hand, you may have hopes that your ex will welcome a pro-child approach … but face it, you may be doing this one on your own for awhile. The "old way" of divorced-parenting is so ingrained that it may take a lot of perseverance on your part for your ex to realize that when it comes to your child, you're not going to be led down that path of bitterness and anger. Repeat that:

"He is not going to lead me down that path. When it comes to my child, I am the parent. I decide how I am going to handle various parenting situations. I am choosing the Pro♡Child Way. And my choice is final. I am not going to be led down that path no matter what bait my ex dangles in front of me."

Your ex knows how to push your buttons. He can bait you without you even realizing it. He knows exactly what to say to get you fired up, defensive, and very angry. I'm sure if given the chance, you have a lot of not-so-pleasant things to say to your ex. Fine, go for it. But not if it has to do with your child. Not if your child can hear you.

When it comes to your child, stuff your ego into the closet and parent from a position of caring. Caring for your child. Of course you love your child. So "caring for your child" should be easy. But when you're standing in the doorway, with your ex screaming at you about something totally irrelevant, it takes more than "caring" to smile and say, "OK! Bye, Daddy, see you tomorrow!" It takes conviction. Conviction that Pro♡Child parenting is what you do.

Sure, setting the parenting tone is a heck of a lot easier with a cooperating ex. But it is worth it to your child for you to go it alone anyway. To your child, one parent who puts her interests and happiness first is better than two parents who only concentrate on defending their egos. Lucky for your child, it only takes **you** to make a significant impact on the divorced-parenting tone. Your child needs you to think of her. Your child needs to hear from you that she is OK and that her dad loves her. She needs to see you smile when in the presence of her dad. She needs to feel your love as a parent, not your hate as an ex.

So even though you would rather scream than smile at your ex, smile anyway. Your smile will change the tone. Your child will immediately sense that she is in a secure place protected by love and understanding for her. And in time, your ex will realize that he's not going to be able to control you anymore. If he's going to interact with you, he's going to have to get used to the fact that you are now parenting the Pro♥Child Way. He'll change his tone, which will greatly benefit your child. Hang onto the vision that someday, he too will put his ego aside and you'll be **parents together.** Until then, remember that you can set the tone, with or without your ex's help.

♥
It takes conviction. Conviction that Pro♥Child parenting is what you do.

Beware of friends and family: They mean well, but only you know what is best for your child.

Talk to friends, get advice from family, read books, listen to counselors, lawyers, and professionals – get all the information that you can, then stop. Stop to think about it all. Stop to think how all of this information affects your child. No matter what they are all saying, it is still you that is in control. And you need to weigh all information before proceeding into action. It may feel great to hear the throngs of supporters championing your side of the divorce, but when it comes to your child, their well-intentioned advice may be off mark. It's very easy to ride the wave of advice, but never abdicate your responsibility to think as a parent. Your child is counting on it.

Everyone gives advice. Your friends are naturally there to tell you all the phrases you want to hear, offering everything from pity parties to war cries. Your lawyer offers legal strategy, procedures, and "next-steps." Your accountant offers formulas and schedules. Fittingly, everyone offers the advice that they are supposed to offer, but that doesn't make their advice the right advice to follow.

Sure, you have every "right" to be angry, sad, frantic, and to take all legal roads available, but when it comes to making your child smile, it may have little to do with what you had the "right" to do. Your child doesn't care that you had a "right" to be hysterical over the visitation exchange, she only cares that all is well through an uneventful good-bye. You may have the "right" to take your ex to court, but your child doesn't want to be at court proceedings, she just wants to be back at school and her activities. You may have the "right" to demand payment from your ex, but your child doesn't care which parent pays for her lesson, she just wants to perform in the recital. Her life is better when it is better at that moment; it is not fair to subject your child to all the turmoil while the "advice" runs its course.

So save your child from your tears, your proceedings, and your accusations.

Tune-out any advice that is vengeful, spiteful, or hurtful towards your ex. The only advice you should listen to is the advice that you would have taken prior to the divorce: advice on how two parents can best nurture, love, and support their child. With so many friends and family members clamoring around you, it is easy to stray from this message. It takes a strong parent to carry the Pro♡Child advice through a divorce. Your child needs you to be strong. Remember, the advice you receive may be well-intentioned, but only you know what is best for your child.

♡ *Tune-out any advice that is vengeful, spiteful, or hurtful towards your ex. The only advice you should listen to is the advice that you would have taken prior to the divorce: advice on how two parents can best nurture, love, and support their child.*

Need to let off steam? Call a friend, not your ex.

Look at it this way, when your ex acts like a jerk, take it as a comforting reminder as to why you got divorced in the first place. After all, when you're divorced, it's probably not best to remember your ex fondly and with longing. Nor should you think of your ex in terms of "Psycho," but your ex's irksome personality traits should make you crack a wise smile – reinforcing your realization that it isn't so bad that you're divorced after all. So, when your ex has a lapse in Pro♡Child parenting and decides the old approach is more satisfying, don't regress with him. Hang up, and call your friend.

"What a jerk! You're not going to believe this…" is great fodder for a girlfriend chat. There is simply nothing more satisfying than your best friend sticking up for your side of the story. Go into all the messy details, explore the juicy alternatives, devise the perfect responses, then laugh it off. Friends are friends because they let you rant and rave, without holding it against you later on. Friends are the perfect remedy for untying that knot in your stomach or for dislodging your foot from your mouth. When you need to let off steam about your ex: call your friend, not your ex.

As time passes, you can help retune your mind from "your ex" into "your child's other parent." We can all agree that "your child's other parent" is a benign term, but "your ex" can send you into that old downward spiral. When your ex is ranting, it can be really hard to think the Pro♡Child Way, so instead of firing back, take time for things to cool down. Granted, things do get easier and less emotional the longer you've been divorced, but wham! just when divorced life is progressing sweetly down that Pro♡Child path, "your child's other parent" becomes "your ex" once again. And boy, is it ever easy to swing back. "What do you mean, I have to drive the whole way and you won't meet us halfway? If that is your attitude, then maybe I just won't bring her at all!" OK, before that comes flying out of your mouth, hopefully you've hung up and dialed your friend.

In your gut, you know when you're crossing outside the Pro♥Child boundary. As you sift through all of your emotions and question if you're being taken advantage of, remember that this isn't about you: it is about your child, and fostering the best relationship between your child and her other parent. If you need to take a chink or two in your pride so that your child can continue to have a good relationship with her parent, then that is easily worth the damage to your pride. Drive your child the extra miles so that she doesn't miss out on time with her dad. You'll never-ever regret doing the right thing for your child. You will regret losing your cool with your ex.

Your ex is your ex for a reason. If he were dependable, thoughtful, or whatever the missing trait, then you'd likely still be married. But you're not. And your ex hasn't all of a sudden developed all those traits that you found him lacking. Maybe your ex is a jerk. Big deal. Call a friend and tell her. But, don't tell your ex in a rampage; and most importantly, don't tell your child. Tell your friend what made your ex such an offensive spouse; tell your child what makes her dad so special.

Whether the incidences happen often or seldom, expect those irrational moments of divorced life. Develop a plan that includes cooling off. Stamp your feet, scream like a banshee, throw a vase, or call a friend. Whatever the response, give yourself time to re-gear towards the Pro♥Child Way.

♥ *When your ex has a lapse in Pro♥Child parenting and decides the old approach is more satisfying, don't regress with him. Hang up, and call your friend.*

Know when you need help: lawyers, police, and mediators.

In your journey through divorce, you will need a lot of help and support. Most of the help you need comes straight out of your gut. Learn to trust what feels right. When weighing important matters, your heart is a good guide down the right path. Sometimes, advice from friends, family, professionals, and lawyers just mixes it all up. But sometimes, your heart knows that without professional advice, your child will suffer. Relying on the advice of a professional may help you achieve your Pro♥Child goal. Just don't call the professional in the old-fashioned way. When you call, make it a Pro♥Child step.

A good lawyer is very important throughout a divorce. But "good" can be defined many different ways. Remember that you are always in control over what your lawyer says and does in your name. Keep your lawyer focused on creating the best path that keeps your child out of the divorce process, not thrown in the midst of it. Resist the "go, fight, win!" attitude. When you are going through the legal steps, take time to pause and reflect, allowing you and your ex time to think and process each step. Know when to take action, but also know when to pause. Take time for the emotions to settle down before proceeding to the next step. It's hard to focus on your child's interests when you're busy protecting yourself.

Mediation is a wonderful tool as you and your ex face tough issues in divorced-parenting. Mediation works towards a solution, not win/lose. Your child deserves a solution. Your child doesn't win when one of her parents loses.

Police are there to protect you or your child from harm. Allowing abuse to your child is not parenting the Pro♡Child Way. There is never an excuse for abuse. If your child is being abused by your ex, call the police and get immediate help.

As a parent, you are the one who is responsible for your child's life. Every day, strive to bring happiness and love to your child. When needed, call on those around you to help.

♡ *When weighing important matters,*
your heart is a good guide
down the right path.

So, if you're so good at being a Pro♡Child parent, why get divorced?

Having an ugly, bitter, drawn-out divorce is so easy. Even friends and family offer constant reminders and ammunition to fuel your negative divorce. It is assumed that the turmoil that was part of your failed marriage will be amplified during your divorce. A nasty public divorce is considered proof that what you must have suffered through was indeed insufferable. Society correlates a nasty divorce to a nasty marriage. But, if you have a Pro♡Child divorce, does it nullify the pain and disappointment that you felt while in the marriage? Nope. Nothing can change what you experienced as you saw your marriage fall apart. I'm sure you've experienced a range of emotions, and not one of them felt good. Living in a failed marriage is soul wrenching.

For whatever reason — good, bad, or ugly — your marriage dissolved. But just because your marriage failed doesn't mean that you are allowed to fail your child at being divorced. More than ever, your child is counting on you to change her environment for the better. She can't do that. You can.

Being married was about you. Being divorced is about your child. A Pro♡Child divorce has no reflection on your marriage. Your marriage is over and in the past – leave it there. Pro♡Child divorced-parenting only reflects the you that has emerged out of a difficult situation. Your child's future is in front of you – shape it. Shape her life to be filled with untarnished love, understanding, patience, security, and smiles.

It takes two to make a marriage succeed. It takes one to be a Pro♡Child divorced parent. Turn around the bad divorce assumptions. Create a new possibility. Make your new role of "divorced parent" a new start for you and your child. Live the Pro♡Child Way.

♡
Just because your marriage failed doesn't mean that you are allowed to fail your child at being divorced.

It's never too late to parent the Pro♡Child Way!

As you are frantically paging through this book, trying to glean some sanity out of an insane situation, you may read a Pro♡Child tip that makes you scoff, "I don't think so!" Thinking the Pro♡Child Way may not come overnight. Let it seep in. Because changing your child's world starts with changing your mindset, and that may take some time. Read and think … re-read and re-think … and then read again, until your "I don't think so!" shrinks away into a "Well, maybe that would be better for my child."

A great first step is your realization that there has to be a better way to parent with an ex. You are not locked into the negative, hateful old spiral of divorce. There is a better way. Next, start contemplating the Pro♡Child Way and start realizing how to apply the Pro♡Child Way in your situations. The last step is to "just do it." Consciously make choices that put your child first – before your reactions of anger, resentment, or sadness towards the divorce.

It is never too late. It doesn't matter how you handled a divorced-parenting situation last year or last week. This book isn't about giving you guilt trips or making you defensive over how you've parented before. It is only about how you can continue to make your child grow in love, comfort, and security from this point on. It is never too late. Keep working on it until you can assert, "That was then, this is now."

You don't need your ex's permission or agreement. You can choose to parent the Pro♡Child Way starting with the next exchange. Gone are the days of the anger-filled meeting. Your smile, your warm greeting to your child, and your

"Bye, Dad!" are now the new norm. Who cares if your ex thinks you're acting ridiculous. It isn't your ex's opinion that matters anymore. Your child is going to think it's great.

The good news is that children are wonderfully resilient and acclimate easily to new attitudes – especially ones that make them smile. It is time for the knot in your child's stomach to disappear. Starting today, make the choice to parent the Pro♡Child Way!

Changing your child's world starts with changing your mindset, and that may take some time.

SECTION I

HERE AND THERE:
Your Child's Comings and Goings as They Relate to Your Ex

A Few Words About Visitation and Holidays

Visitation schedules, holiday schedules, dealing with your ex over and over again … when it comes to your child's comings and goings, it's easy for her to get lost in the emotional shuffle. Divorce is wrought with ugliness; divorced-parenting is exhausting. You wake up every day with the best of intentions, but somewhere between your ex being late again and your child's missing pajamas, your nerves are shot. Your ex has sabotaged another day. There are many possible pits, bumps, and roadblocks that arise when it comes to visitation and holidays. But how you handle these every-day, every-week, over-and-over-again occurrences are significant to your child's well-being.

Regroup, refocus, and remind yourself the purpose behind it all: your child. Your ex may be all the rotten things you say, but does he love his child? Does he wake up in the morning with the best of intentions for his child? Most likely, the answers are, "Yes." Keep plugging away, and make it work for your child's best interest. For every divorced-parenting situation, there are two solutions: one is to react to your ex, the other is to create a better environment for your child. You can significantly impact the tone. Take each situation and turn it into a positive experience for your child.

Remember, "It's not about you, it's about your child." Your child's comings and goings as they relate to your ex can either end in disaster for your child, or can be part of a smooth, loving relationship. It is up to you to choose the right tone. Throughout your parenting decisions, constantly reiterate that your child is important and loved by both parents – regardless of what your ego may think about your ex. You greatly influence your child's picture. All that is important is that your child thinks her other parent is wonderful.

Think of your child in terms of experiences, not minutes. Regardless of the amount of time that you or your ex may spend with your child, make each moment count. A quality relationship with your child isn't dependent on the quantity of time. Your child doesn't need equal time, she needs equal love: and that love can be expressed in many ways that are better than counting minutes. It is possible for a child that only sees her one parent occasionally to have a more fulfilling relationship than a child who sees her parent frequently. Of course, it would be wonderful if you could spend many minutes with your child, but that isn't always the best arrangement for your child. The amount of time you spend with your child should be guided by what is best for her, not by your selfish needs to just "have her more."

It is even possible for your child to have a better relationship with her other parent after the divorce than before the divorce. Think back to all those harried moments prior to your divorce. Work, meals, chores, errands, and stress may have kept your ex from spending quality time with your child. Now, through structured visitation, your child may be able to spend more quality time than ever with her other parent. Playground or pool time may replace the prior avoidance times, allowing for a more contented child and parent. It's all how you look at it.

Divorce is something that your child will always live with, you might as well make it positive. When it comes to visitation and holidays, choose to parent the "Pro♥Child Way." It is an opportunity for you to reveal how two parents can love one child so very much. As I always say: "What does divorce have to do with anything?"

♥
Your child doesn't need equal time, she needs equal love: and that love can be expressed in many ways that are better than counting minutes.

3

Divorced Situation ▮

VISITATION: Determining the Time-Split

After a separation or divorce, one of the first issues to determine is the time-split. In other words: How much time is your child spending with each parent? And no, the answer is not an automatic "equal." This is an important issue, a potentially tough obstacle when you and your ex are fresh from the emotional grinder. Remember to keep your child's needs first. Your needs and your ex's needs are not your child's needs. Here are two possible time-split schedules; will you follow the Old Way or choose the Pro♥Child Way?

The *Old* Way

For the whole of your child's life, *you* were the one who took care of her moment-by-moment needs. *You* were the one who did the everyday, seemingly insignificant, routine caregiving that formed your child into a functioning and thriving child. *You* were the one that your child expected during times of distress, whether in the middle of the night or the middle of the day. And now where will your child be? Spending half her time away from the parent that she counted on most.

Sure, her other parent was in the picture too, but when put to the test, you are clearly the parent who was by her side as the routine of life unfolded. You are her "there-for parent." It's just the way parenthood unfolded in your household. And when you were married, your child's dad was just fine with it that way! He was quite content to turn potty training over to you. Now, he's morphed into "Super Dad!" wanting to share it all. In fact, not only is he now demanding "half" of her time, he's implying that he's always been equally involved! Yeah. You don't *think* so! This history rewrite is getting out of hand.

Of course your ex loves your child and of course she will be safe when at his house. And you don't deny all of the activities that they did together and, you rationalize, it's only fair that he gets to have her equally. "Equal" is just the consequence of divorce, or so they say. While a part of you thinks that halving-it could be the "right" thing to do (even slightly revengeful for all of your missed nights' sleep), it just isn't natural. You wonder why you are all pretending that the parenting was equal before the divorce? It just isn't the way your household has been. It just isn't the way you've both brought up your daughter. Equal is not what your child has experienced, and if asked, equal isn't how she sees it.

♡ *A thoughtful time-split schedule starts by considering the needs of your child.*

The *Pro ♥ Child* **Way**

Before you subscribe to the notion that your child should spend equal time with both of her parents, take time to think. Perhaps it will be the best solution, perhaps not. But with any arrangement concerning your child, your child deserves a thought-filled solution. Above all, your child needs to feel security. Security that her needs will be met. Met consistently and with love.

Depending on your child's age, "needs" can come in many forms. For a teenager, the need may be for privacy and a taxi to and from activities. For a toddler, the needs are numerous and life-dependent.

A thoughtful time-split schedule starts by considering the needs of your child. This is where your discussions begin. Your child's life is too important to just "wing-it" after the time-split decision has been made. First, start by listing and agreeing to what your child's needs are. After that, you can be more truthful about whether each parent is comfortable really meeting these needs.

Can you be available after school for your teenager who needs to be picked up and taken to her lesson? What about her weekend babysitting job or her youth group activities? Are you available to take her to those? And what about a quiet place in your house where she can do her calculus homework and unwind after a stressful day? What about the late-night meltdown that involves tears and horrific stories of peer pressure? Can you handle those? Your child has real needs.

Before subscribing to the equal time-split, make sure you can equally take on these responsibilities. Your rising blood pressure is a good indicator that all of these needs may be beyond your abilities. Take a breath and allow in some space. If your child's other parent would be better at handling some of these needs, then admit it. Or, if you suspect that your ex can't handle these issues, address it. Your child is likely freaking out over any suspect arrangements. Your teenager doesn't need more stress. Ask her what concerns she has with the time-split schedule and then address those concerns with your ex in a non-confrontational way.

Is your teenager stressed about doing her homework at both houses? Maybe the solution is for her to spend most of the weeknights at one house. Or maybe the solution is to buy her a laptop computer, double office supplies, and a desk in a quiet part of both houses. Your child deserves to have her concerns answered. A new 15" MacBook Pro isn't a bribe, it's a tool that may make the difference in determining the best time-split schedule. Of course, an excited squeal from your child is also positive! Once you and your ex have decided on the schedule, include your child so that she can hear how her needs will be met. Your child wins when her parents realize what is best for her and then do it.

Younger children have a different set of needs. A child who grows up knowing that their needs will be met, grows up feeling secure and loved. This security is formed the day she is born. While both you and your ex have been involved, likely one of you took the nurturing lead while the other parent may have taken the lead in other areas of household life. Perhaps you were able to equally share the parenting, finances, and home life, but most families find an arrangement that works better. Equal isn't always better. It is unusual for spouses to really split the parenting role equally. Ask yourself: Who was the primary nurturer or "there-for parent"? If unknown, ask the pediatrician, the babysitter, the school teacher, the playground group, the neighbor, the grandparents, or the friends. In an instant, they will tell you which of you was the "there-for parent."

Once you and your ex are honest about who your child turned to for routine life, you're at the starting point of the time-split discussion.

So do it! Determine which parent has been the "there-for parent." The younger the child, the more time that child will need with her "there-for parent." It is your goal to minimize the stress that your child feels as a child of divorce. Her stress is directly tied to how she perceives her needs will be met. If she feels that her needs won't be properly met when with her other parent, then you'll have a stressed child. Sure, parental roles can develop, expand, and change. But in the beginning of the divorce, "what is" is what should be. As you all mature in your divorced roles, the time-split may change. This may happen over weeks, months, or years. One day, the time-splits may even be fully reversed. This isn't a goal. There are no time-split goals. The only goal is that your child can relax knowing that her needs are being met and that she is loved by both parents.

By establishing a history-based time-split schedule, you are meeting two important needs of your child. First, her need to have a secure "home base" where her "there-for parent" will continue to be there for her. And second, time with her other parent where they can expand their relationship. It's so important to the life of your child that she gets to experience time and love from both of her parents. The amount of love shared cannot be measured by the amount of time spent.

If you are the "there-for parent," examine your child's needs and discern how your ex can expand his abilities to handle these needs over time. If your ex is the "there-for parent," honor your child's need to be wrapped in the comfort of that tradition, and don't pretend that overnight you can now be the parent that you haven't been. Realize that it will be a process of learning — you learning how to further be involved in meeting your child's needs, and your child learning that she can now rely on you too. You are not "giving in" when you're honoring your child's life as it has been. Instead, be grateful that your child has had a parent that has been "there-for" her throughout the years, and embrace the moments that you will continue to create together.

Determining the time-split arrangement is not a one-time, one-size solution. Ask the questions. Give honest answers. And involve your ex in a structured, positive conversation that focuses on finding solutions to your child's needs. Acknowledge each other's strengths and encourage parental growth for your child's sake. Affirm that as you all change, so may the time-split schedule. Keep the mind of a parent, while looking through your child's heart.

Divorced Situation 2

VISITATION: Setting the Visitation Schedule

Once you and your ex have agreed on the time-split that is best for your child, the next issue comes on its heels: determining the visitation schedule. Take a deep breath and keep plugging away. Take heart that your child can thrive when a thoughtful plan is developed. Here are two possible visitation schedules; will you follow the Old Way or choose the Pro♥Child Way?

The *Old* Way

Grab the aspirin, the calendar, and your pencil – it's time to play "figuring out this month's schedule!" First, the starting point: Your ex had visitation last weekend ... no, that was your weekend, so that means this next weekend is your ex's weekend, yours is the weekend after that. So for this month, the 4th and 18th are his; the 11th and 25th are yours. As you're staring at the calendar, you feel dread coming over you as you think about planning a vacation for next year. Where did you put next year's calendar anyway? Is the second weekend in July your weekend or your ex's weekend? Ah forget it, you think, as you push aside the family cruise brochure.

And then you open the mail to find two birthday party invitations for your child. **Crud**. On Saturday the 5th, will your child be spending the day with you or your ex? And what about the other party? Where will she be then? Do you need to call your ex about the first party, the second party, or both? Maybe it's just easier if your child didn't go at all.

Next you think about your child's homework project that is due at the end of the semester. It will require some last-minute preparations. Will your child be able to do that in her room at your home where all of the project pieces are? Or will you have to make arrangements for it to happen while she is at your ex's house. You sigh as you think of your child trying to reorganize it all.

As the aspirin starts to dull your headache, you begin to reflect back on how this schedule came to be. During the rush to "get things settled," the "every-other" schedule just happened. You didn't even question it. You just wanted it to be finished. Besides, isn't it what everyone does?

♥ *Consistency, frequency, and clarity of schedule should mold your visitation arrangement.*

The *Pro ♥ Child* Way

Growing up, your child should never question where she will be on any given night. She shouldn't have to think about it. She should be secure and comforted knowing where she will be on any Monday, Tuesday, Wednesday, Thursday, etc. She should know where she'll be every second weekend in July and every third Sunday of January. Prior to the divorce, your child never had to look at a calendar to see where she was sleeping. While divorce does bring adjustments, the basic foundations of your child's life don't need to change. Your child should not feel the uncertainty that comes with an "every-other" schedule.

This uncertainty about the future discourages long-term planning – for your child, for you, and for your ex. Why bother thinking about two months from now when the basic starting point of "where I'll be sleeping" can't even be determined? Should your nine-year-old sign up for the church sleepover? Before she even considers all the complicated nine-year-old reasons to participate or not, she needs to figure out if she'll be with Mom or Dad that weekend. Your daughter's book report is due at the end of the month and she prefers to work in her room at Mom's house. Does the last weekend of the month correspond with "Mom's weekend" or "Dad's weekend"? Why bother trying to figure it out? Planning for the future becomes more trouble than it's worth. The "every-other" solution to visitation becomes the problem.

Especially for young children, "every-other" just doesn't work. Young children don't process time like adults do. We've all been there: the seemingly endless car ride to Grandma's; the "can you play with me now?" a full 30 seconds after you've explained that you can play after unloading the dishwasher. If 30 seconds is incomprehensible, imagine what every-other weekend with Dad feels like to your young child. It might as well be every-other year. Your child needs more frequent reminders that she is loved and cared for by both parents. Avoid the "every-other" schedule.

What is best for your child when it comes to the visitation schedule? Your goal is to instill routine and a consistent presence of love from each parent.

Arrange your visitation schedule so that your child spends time more frequently with each parent. For the young child the length of time with each parent is not as important as the frequency of time. A frequent, clear schedule will quickly establish a routine that your child can remember, but this can only be accomplished if you are consistent. Consistency is key in creating a foundation of security. Consistency, frequency, and clarity of schedule should mold your visitation arrangement.

With the proper time-split in mind, create a schedule that includes consistent, frequent visits with the other parent. The schedule should be fixed on named days of the week and events, not based on "every-other." For example, every Friday, dinner and sleepover with Dad. Every Tuesday after school. Every Saturday after breakfast to past dinner with Mom. Every Monday, Wednesday, and Friday early evenings with Dad. Look at your child's schedule and then at her dad's and your schedules. What arrangement can you stick to? If Dad's work schedule frequently takes him away on business during the week, then don't arrange weekday visits. If he is back on Friday, then a Friday-night-to-Saturday-noon-plus-all-day-Sunday schedule might work best. If both parents live in the same school district, consider a weeknight visit.

Just like the time-split schedule, keep in mind that your child's needs change with passing time and passing seasons. Perhaps overnight weekday visits are disruptive to your child during the school year, but a welcome treat during the summer. Perhaps being at Dad's all day Tuesday was possible when she was young, but as age and interests expanded, your school-age child is now involved in soccer after school and ballet in the evening, leaving little time for Dad except in the car. Realizing this isn't enough time with her dad, you both change the schedule so that Dad can be the taxi on Wednesdays as well. It isn't much, but at least it doubles the chance for connection. Don't underestimate the value of frequency. It's shocking how much you can learn from your teenager in a car ride, in contrast to silence at the dinner table.

Be an "every" parent, not an "every-other" parent. And then stick to it. Custody arrangements aren't a goal; they're a daily, monthly, yearly process. Consider your child's schedule, consider your own schedule and your ex's schedule, and arrange a consistent schedule that you all can keep. Your child is counting on you.

Divorced Situation 3

VISITATION: Helping Your Child's Adjustment

Now that your child's visitation schedule is in place, it's time to put it into action. Simply letting it "just happen" will have disastrous results for your child. Instead, you need to guide the visitation routines. The best starting place is at the beginning, and that means the beginning of the visitation. Long before your child drives off in your ex's car, the adjustment routines need to begin. Depending on the route you choose, this beginning could go smoothly for your child or end in tears. How will you choose to guide your child through her visitation adjustment?

The *Old* Way

OMG! Will this day never end? The phone is ringing, the dog is barking, the TV is blaring, and your house is a mess. Not to mention that your child has not taken her nap and it's feeling like a very long day. As you're running around in a tizzy, your ex appears for his night of visitation. Great … just his being there raises your stress. As you're scrambling to put a wiggling child into shoes and a coat, your child freaks and the scene erupts. As you frantically shove her belongings into a bag, you glare at your ex. He has no idea what you go through! Can't he see how completely overwhelmed and stressed you are? A typical disastrous start to your child's visitation, and it's all your ex's fault. You close the door relieved that he's gone.

Visits with Mom and Dad are wonderful times that should be naturally flowing, positive experiences for your child. Help your child adjust to her visit so that she can enjoy it.

The *Pro* ♥ *Child* Way

Visitation should not be an emotional production. Any person would be upset if one moment they were playing and the next they were being whisked out the door. Your child deserves more consideration than that. Take time, and help your child adjust. Prepare your child for her visitation so that she does not feel surprised, unprepared, or interrupted. Take time to remind her that it is happening, help her get ready, and entertain her with "waiting for Dad" activities.

Your child needs security in knowing what she will be doing and when. Tell your child about her upcoming visitation with her other parent. Remind her of the visitation the day before, the night before, that morning, during that day, and as the hour approaches. Never let a visitation be a surprise. Instead, teach your child to expect her visit so that she will learn to plan and prepare for it.

The process of preparing isn't just to collect a bunch of things, it is to prepare her caring heart. Once your child knows of her upcoming visit, help her prepare for it. Create routines that are reserved for visitation days. Pull out her special traveling bag and have her think what she wants to pack. Perhaps this week's items include a drawing, a rock treasure, a favorite stuffed animal, or a book. Be sure to include all necessities, including clothes and shoes.

Talk about how nice her visit will be. You want your child to look forward to her visits. Start by erasing any guilt that she may have about "leaving you alone." Don't let your child think that you will be sad without her. Let her know that you are happy that she is going to be spending time with Dad. Knowing that you are upbeat about the visit will have a positive effect on your child's attitude. Lastly, in talking with your child, sprinkle in the phrase "get to," as in "You are so lucky that you get to spend time with Dad." It makes the visitation sound much more special.

Now that the preparations are complete, it's time to wait for Dad. This is not the time for your child to start a TV program, video game, or any activity where the completion may not coincide with Dad's arrival. "Waiting for Dad" activities can be any number of games that can stop at a moment's notice. "Simon Says," playing catch, and I Spy™ are great "waiting for Dad" games.

Don't disregard these important transition rituals just because your child is older. Your pre-teen may not need a cartoon-character overnight bag, but she still needs you to help the transition flow. So plop on her bed while she gathers up some things and chat on the front porch while waiting for Dad. Show respect for her and her dad by taking time out of your busy schedule to make this work.

Divorced Situation 4

VISITATION: Packing for the Visit

An essential step in preparing your child for a successful visit is the routine of packing. Not only does this assure that your child will have her things, but also prepares her mind and heart for the upcoming transition. Packing can become a cherished time for you and your child, as you sit giggling on the bedroom floor, filling her pack with special items. Or, packing can be a missed opportunity to prepare your child for her upcoming visit. Will packing be included or forgotten in your child's routine?

The Old Way

Your child's stuff isn't cheap. You managed to buy her clothes that she'll wear. You bought her sparkly toothpaste and the race-car toothbrush that she wanted. You even found shoes that fit her and that she likes. You are the one that searched for the perfect cuddly, stuffed bunny and you don't want it going to your ex's house! No way are all these things ending up lost.

He should get off his bum and hit the stores like you did. You've bought the things necessary for your house. He needs to buy what is necessary for his house. If he forgot something that your child needs, then he'll just have to go out and buy it – like you do all of the time. Maybe next time, he'll learn to be more prepared. Maybe next time, he'll realize that she really does need pajamas, underwear, and shoes. Her whining should be good motivation for him. After all, your child isn't going on vacation: why should she pack?

What is the point of all this ado?
Through the routine ...
your child will smile.

The *Pro♥Child* Way

Whether it is for a few hours or overnight, packing for your child's visitation is an essential step. It's easy to rationalize that your ex should be prepared for your child's visit. After all, he knows that she is coming. Setting your ex up for disaster does have its appeal, but don't let your child be the casualty.

Start by having your child help you select a "traveling bag." This bag can be either a purchased one displaying her favorite TV character or a homemade bag that is personalized just for her. In either case, your child knows that this is a special bag that is used when she gets to be with her dad.

Prior to each visitation, have your child help you fill the bag. Be sure to include needed items such as a change of clothes. While your child may have some extra clothes at Dad's, it is your responsibility as a parent to see that she has something to put on in the morning. If she ends up not wearing the outfit, fine, but at least she knows that it is available in her pack. Be sure to include some fun pajamas. There is something special for your child to have fun pajamas that are "just for Dad's house." As time passes and tensions ease between you and your ex, you can work towards having two sets of essentials at each home. Until then, pack all your child's needs. Two toothbrushes never hurt anyone.

Your child should be instrumental in selecting the special items that travel to Dad's house. If stuffed animals are the favorite toy, help your child select which animal "gets to go" to Dad's house. It will please you to see her reward her animals in this way. The days prior to your child's visit will inevitably produce a found treasure or painting that is to be shared with Dad. Be sure to include your child's treasures and creations.

When peering into your child's pack and wincing over all that is ready to disappear out your door, remember this important point: It isn't your stuff. It is your child's book, doll, pajamas, and hairbrush. These are your child's things, and she has every right to expect that her things go where she goes … even to Dad's house. If after several visits, you notice that her sock drawer is looking empty, give Dad a private call to see if you can pick her things up. Washed or unwashed only matters to your ego; your child could care less if Mom or Dad does the washing. With a smile on your face, wash, fold, and prepare her things for another round. Your child is worth it.

What is the point of all this ado? Through the routine of packing and the special emphasis that is placed on items for Dad, your child will smile. Any insecurity about leaving is now overshadowed by "special pajamas" and treasures for Dad. Packing for your child's visit with Dad is important. Take time with your child to develop this special routine.

Divorced Situation 5

VISITATION: The Tearful Goodbye

As your child leaves with your ex for her visit, tears may flow. But are these tears a constant reaction to her parents' antics or are they just the occasional bump on the way through childhood? You can create an atmosphere where your child can lovingly move from one household to another. Or you can flame the fires of stress and uncertainty for your child resulting in an emotional, tearful goodbye. It all depends on which way you choose.

The *Old* Way

Here it comes again: the visitation exchange. You take a deep breath, but the clock is making its way towards visitation hour and you're dreading it. The tension in your neck is getting worse and the pit in your stomach is growing. Why can't your child just stay home? Everything is going so well and her leaving just messes it all up.

Your friends all think that you're so lucky – having "free time" without your child. Time to yourself to do and go wherever you want. But what you're feeling has nothing to do with pleasure. You hate all parts of this: hate seeing your ex, hate listening to his sarcasm, hate letting go of your child, hate seeing her leave, hate being alone. With every thought, you hold your child closer.

The moment that your ex arrives, you instinctively clasp your arms around your child, as if to protect her from what's about to come. With every nerve, you wish you could make this not happen. You look into her eyes and apologetically confess that it is time for her to go away. On cue, your child disintegrates into panic. With her arms clenched tight around your neck and her sobs increasing, you just glare at your ex. Can't he see that he should just go away! Can't he see all the turmoil that he causes!

Waiting for some sign that he'll just give up and go away, you hang on to your child. And wait. And wait. Finally, he pries her away, leaving you empty. As you listen to her screams, you close your eyes and cringe at the lifetime of visitations to come.

♡ *You are responsible for setting a positive tone for your child.*

The *Pro ♥ Child* Way

Leave the dramatics out of it and focus on what is best for your child. What is best for your child is to see a smiling face picking her up and a smiling face waving goodbye. This quick exchange should be free of tension between the parents and solely focused on the child.

With your child's special suitcase ready at the door and her coat on, the last step is ***watching.*** Your ex's presence shouldn't be a surprise to your child. Even if it's only a few seconds, your child needs that moment – from her Dad driving-in to his walking up the walk – to transition her mind. And you also need that time to compose yourself.

As your ex is pulling up to the house, you and your child should be looking out the window. "Look, there's Daddy driving in!" you should exclaim. (Repeat to yourself: "Focus on my child, not my ex.") And with that, grab her prepared things, open the door, and wait outside. Waiting outside is important, especially if you are in the early stages of divorce. That way, you aren't pinned inside your house with your ex.

As your ex is approaching, wave cheerfully. It doesn't matter if you would rather see him run over by a car ... this is for your child's sake. You are responsible for setting a positive tone for your child. Your child will momentarily be leaving with this person, and she isn't going to go quietly if she senses something is wrong. So wave and create an inviting atmosphere for your ex's arrival.

When greeting your ex, do so through your child by exclaiming, "Hi Daddy!" Quickly add a quick comment like, "Wait till you see the nice surprise that she has for you in her pack." Make it a positive statement that focuses on your child. This is not the time to be sarcastic, rude, or comment on the divorce. Likewise, ignore any negative statements made by your ex. Keep smiling and focused on your child. The only goal is to have your child leave quickly while smiling. Initiate the departure by turning and going back into the house. Be sure to send your child off with an upbeat, "Bye-bye! I love you. See you tomorrow!" Leave the soap-opera style tears and clinging emotions out of it. How could that possibly help your child? Instead, smile and wave good-bye from inside the window.

Your child needs to be reassured that her parents are in control. A young child is comforted knowing that her parents are making the best decisions for her. In this instance, the "best decision" is the visitation schedule that you and your ex arranged. Be confident that the schedule was well thought-out and stick to it. The visitation schedule should not be determined by the child.

Will there ever be tears? Sure. Tears happen – for many different reasons, just make sure that your antics aren't the cause. When tears flow, acknowledge that you can see that she is sad. Reassure her that you love her and that you'll be smiling knowing that she's having fun with Dad. Even during full-blown hysterics, stick to the plan. Go back into the house and leave the situation to your ex. A call ten minutes later should confirm that her smiles have returned.

After several consistent visits and exchanges, she will learn that her moods will not manipulate the visitation schedule. After several consistent visits, it will also get easier for you and your ex.

Divorced Situation **6**

VISITATION: The End of a Visit

You've determined the visitation schedule, you've created routines, you've packed, you've waved goodbye: now is the ordeal over? Not for your child. The end of her visit requires as much attention as the steps leading up to it. "It ain't over till it's over," and you still have more smiling to do. So take this opportunity to show your child how much you care for her and her feelings. You can welcome your child home, or you can waste this opportunity by glaring at your ex. Which will you choose?

The *Old* Way

You've had the whole time that your child has been gone to steam, rehash, and worry. Your thoughts have been equally divided between what a louse your ex has been to you and what an incompetent father he is continuing to be to your child. You can only imagine that she's been looking at the clock too, waiting for the visit to end so that she can return back to you. You shake your head and sneer as you think of him.

As he drives up you can't help but stare at him. As he gets closer, you go out and wait for him, maybe looking at your watch and scowling to add some effect. Once again, you seize another opportunity to demonstrate how on-top-of-things you are and how totally lacking he is. Can't he ever be on time? For added effect you add, "You're late," and delve into all the times that his irresponsibility has caused problems. As your child escapes away from both of you, you stand your ground, being sure to get in the last word.

Finally, he retreats and you're able to get on to the next item of your day's to-do list. With your child in hand, the "I should have said" circles in your mind. You're hoping that next time you'll be more clever in your responses to him.

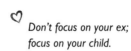

Don't focus on your ex;
focus on your child.

The *Pro ♥ Child* Way

Stop glaring, sighing, and gritting your teeth as your ex hands over your child. As you face your ex at the end of a visit, your mind may be running a checklist of his offenses, but it is what shows on the outside of your face that matters to your child. At the end of the visit exchange, don't focus on your ex; focus on your child. What does your child need from you? She needs a smile, a warm greeting, and help saying "good-bye" to her dad.

When the time approaches for your child to come home, drop everything and be waiting. By seeing you waiting, your child will see how important she really is to you. If you're at home, your child should see you at the front door, awaiting her arrival. Open the door and wait for her there. If your exchange is in a parking lot or other public place, be there first, waiting with a smile and an enthusiastic wave directed at your child. Be mindful that your smile doesn't fade with each passing minute. You should be welcoming, no matter how late your ex may be.

It's important for your ex to help your child out of his car and up to the house or into your car. It's also important that you stay put. This allows for your ex and child to close their visit and transition. It also allows you to close the door and not get dragged into an ex-exchange.

Once your child is with you, give her a hug and say, "Hi, sweetie!" Keep in mind that exaggerated professions of missing her sends the wrong message. Don't make your child feel that you have been sad and worried while she has been with her dad. A simple "Welcome home!" is warm and welcoming. A teary-eyed, sing-songy "I've missssssed youuuuu!" is way too much for your child to handle. Likewise, avoid any dramatics towards your ex. Don't question him. Don't scrutinize him. In fact, you don't even have to look at him. Stay focused on your child. You're almost done, hang in there.

Last on the list are the "good-byes." Just as your child should greet her dad at the beginning of the visit, so should she also say good-bye to him. Depending on the age of your child, you may be the one saying it for her. So, as your ex is walking back to the car, be sure to say, "Bye, Dad! Love ya, Dad! See you on Friday!" and help your child wave good-bye and blow kisses. Remember that this should be done with a smile on your face. With that, another successful visit is done.

Divorced Situation **7**

VISITATION: Waiting for the Inevitable Late Pick-Up

The schedule has been set and your child's time with her dad is about to start, and here you both sit, waiting. As the minutes tick by, where is your focus? Is it on your growing resentment of an ex that is late? Or can you step back and reassure your child that she is loved just the same? Choose to teach your child understanding and that love is not diminished by a traffic jam.

The *Old* Way

It's the end of a long day and you and your child are staring out the window, waiting for her father to show up. Your ex is late picking up your child. As each minute passes, your child becomes more restless and you become more resentful. Your sighs become heavier with each labored glance at your watch. Typical, you think.

Doesn't this just prove how insensitive he is? How many times has he left you waiting? And waiting. And waiting. It's all about him. It's always been all about him. He could care less about your schedule. In fact, he's probably doing this on purpose just to piss you off.

And how hard is it to predict how long it takes to drive from point A to point B? Come on! This isn't the virgin trip. The road didn't suddenly become longer. Anyone would be able to plan better than what your ex did. Your girlfriend is going to roll her eyes when you tell her how irresponsible he was *again.*

Sure, you hate to see you child witness how insensitive her father is, but it's not your fault he's late. There's nothing you can do about it, and besides, the sooner she realizes what a louse he is, the better.

♡ *When you are waiting for the inevitable late pick-up, your child needs reassurance that she is important and loved.*

The *Pro* ♥ *Child* **Way**

Often when your ex is late, you are unprepared and left wondering if he will ever show up. The "waiting for Dad" games are great for a couple of minutes, but they were never meant to last a half-hour. Although it may be more fun for you to think evil thoughts, your ex's delay could have more to do with traffic than being irresponsible. You just don't know.

When you are waiting for the inevitable late pick-up, your child needs reassurance that she is important and loved. "Did Daddy forget about me?" "Is Daddy doing something more fun than being with me?" Your child may not be saying this aloud, but certainly these are thoughts that are probably running through her mind, as well as yours.

Sometimes, parents are late. Your child isn't dumb. She realizes when her dad is late. Don't let her fret and wonder. Instead, talk to your child. Acknowledge that her dad is late, reassure her that it has nothing to do with her, and redirect her thoughts to other activities.

Chances are, you may not know the exact cause, but traffic is a pretty good guess. Look at your child and say to her, "I bet Dad is sitting in a traffic jam, wishing he was sitting here with you instead. We'll just wait until he gets here." Even if you have your doubts, this is the story and you should stick to it. It does your child no good to hear your other theories on Dad's late arrival.

If your ex is really late, casually put on the local traffic reports. You may be surprised to hear that there really is a road closing on his route! By sharing this information with your child, you both will be able to wait it out better.

During these special circumstances, it's OK for your child to take off her coat and become involved in a longer project. Just be sure to tell your child that as soon as Dad pulls up, her activity or game has to stop.

When Dad does arrive, be sure to greet him in the normal smiling way and suggest that the traffic must have been *really* bad and that he must have been worried thinking about her waiting for him. Wave good-bye and turn away.

When the occasional late pick-up becomes chronic, it is time to reassess the visitation schedule. **Privately** discuss the schedule with your ex and determine if a time change is needed. Why? Because no one wants to feel forgotten, especially your child.

Divorced Situation 8

VISITATION: Asking Questions vs. Prying

Juicy details about your ex: isn't that the fringe benefit of your child's visit with her other parent? Resist the information-temptation. Show your child that you're interested in her, not her other parent.

The *Old* Way

Your child is barely in the door and already you are anxious to hear about her time with Dad. Did she eat properly? What time did she go to bed? Has she taken a bath? Did she brush her teeth? In other words, "How badly did Dad mess up this time?"

The questions continue: What did her father say? Did he say anything about you? What does he do all day? Who did they see? Was another woman there? In other words, is he failing without you?

As you've waited for your child's return, you've fantasized about the promising juicy information. You've had so much fun speculating about the who, what, where, and when of your ex's life, always drawing conclusions of how his current behavior relates to you. You're eagerly awaiting the next episode of "Life at Dad's" so that you can learn about what he is thinking and doing. Oh, if only it was simultaneously broadcasted on TV, then you would have all of your questions answered and your suspicions confirmed.

With giddy anticipation, you pour yourself a cup of coffee and welcome your child home. The goods are about to be delivered and you're settling back to enjoy all the details. Let the interrogation begin!

♡ *By being given the freedom to express her thoughts and experiences when and how she wants, your child learns that it is safe for her to share.*

The *Pro ♥ Child* **Way**

Give your child some space, especially when she first comes home from a visit. Let her unwind from the experience by helping her unpack or letting her dillydally. Stay available but not intrusive.

Instead of prying, create an environment that encourages your child to tell you about her feelings and experiences. Set the groundwork for open communication. Start by telling her about your day: grocery shopping (where you saw a friend) and walking the dog (who barked at a squirrel). Keep things loose so that your child can ask questions or respond. You can then ask the open-ended question, "Tell me about your day!" Chances are, you still won't get much of a response, but it lets your child know that you are interested in what she has to say.

Most of the "answers" that you'll receive will come when you aren't expecting them. When your child announces, "I baked cookies with Joanne at Dad's house!", choke down your initial reaction of "***Who?***" Instead, somehow manage to respond, "That sounds yummy, what kind?" Don't pry. It will probably be several more visits and even more cryptic messages from your child until you find out that Joanne is a lady friend of her dad. Even though you may want to know more about the mystery lady, your child only wants you to know that she was having fun. And in the end, all you really need to know is that she is having fun and is being treated well.

If you have true questions over your child's comments, discuss it privately with your ex. Your conversation should be focused and non-threatening. "Our daughter mentioned that she has been having fun with Joanne. Is now a good time for you to tell me who that is?" Being able to respond appropriately to your child shows her that you cared and were paying attention to her comments.

If you start drilling for answers the moment your child walks in the door, you will most likely get silence, or worse, you'll get sarcasm. Your child knows the reasons behind the questions. It becomes apparent whether you're asking for her sake or for yours.

By giving her the freedom to express her thoughts and experiences when and how she wants, your child learns that it is safe for her to share with you – that she can relay her thoughts, concerns, and silly stories without the retaliation of your questions. Treat your child's comments as sweet drops of sharing. Leave the twenty questions alone, and focus on your child and what she wants to share with you.

Divorced 9
Situation

VISITATION: Different Places, Different Routines

You and your ex have agreed on a visitation schedule. You've helped your child prepare her bag, and the good-byes have been said. Now your thoughts are preoccupied with her actually being at the other home. Is your ex prepared to handle this visit? Will your child's needs be taken care of? What is your part in seeing that things go right at his house? How can you ensure that her routines won't be disturbed? The bad news: *You can't.* The good news: *Your child will be fine.*

The Old Way

"Fine," you think. Maybe you do have to deal with your child visiting *him.* Maybe you do have to accept that she has to *do time* at your ex's house. But you'll be darned if you're going to let him mess up the carefully planned routines that you have put in place making your child's new life normal. You realize that the divorce caused your child stress, and "normal" is now being had come hell or high water.

What is normal? Well "normal" is Norman Rockwell. A full breakfast at the kitchen table with pleasant music and light conversation. A bedtime routine that includes a bath, then pajamas, followed by a snack, teeth-brushing, a story, then "I Love Yous." Oh, and the "I Love Yous" have to include Grammy, Nana, Mommy, Daddy, and the dog and the cat. In that order. Normal is going to get your child through this divorce. And normal will be instituted — here and there!

You've worked very hard at establishing routines that are good for your child. And just ask anyone who knows, your ex is definitely not going to come up with this on his own. He needs to be "enlightened" and you're just the person to ensure that it happens. He will implement the routines, and your child's life will go as planned by you.

So, you start: notes instructing your ex on how your daughter should brush her teeth; emails that detail the bedtime routine; endless phone calls that lay out everything from how she should set the table to how she should get dressed. You keep your notepad close. You're going to make sure that your child's needs are met — here and there!

So "fine," maybe you still don't like that she's gone. But through your hard work, at least you know that she'll survive. Your ex should thank you for all your effort. Does he? Of course not, but preserving the routines is worth his snide remarks and his flaring temper. You really could care less what he thinks. Face it, "some people do it differently." Children adapt. Children thrive.

The *Pro ♥ Child* **Way**

Quit micromanaging every detail of your child's life at her dad's house. Concentrate on establishing and carrying out routines for your child at your house, not your ex's.

These endless discussions between you and your ex concerning your child's routines cause arguments and stress, all in the name of trying to maintain a better environment for your child. Yes, the routines may become regimented in that process, but instead of creating a better environment for your child, all you create is parental stress and resentment in carrying out someone else's plans. Your child does not need a home filled with resentment, she needs a home filled with love.

Children are very adaptable and smart. They know that different places have different routines. They can understand that Mom has a different way of doing things than Dad does. At Mom's house, the bedtime routine includes "lights out" talks, while at Dad's house, "story time" is the routine. It doesn't matter that these routines are different. Your child will figure out that at Mom's house it is done one way, and at Dad's house another way. Even within households where both parents live, you'll see differences between Mom's and Dad's routines. Face it, "some people do it differently." Children adapt. Children thrive.

"But, what about…," you protest. Resist the temptation to intervene. Your child will survive. This isn't about life and death issues. This is about brushing teeth, TV watching, dinnertime, and doing chores. If your ex's approach isn't quite up to your standard, acknowledge it with your child. "I know dad does things differently, but that doesn't change the fact that he and I both love you the same. I'm glad that you get to spend time there." Yes, it is possible for those words to come out of your mouth. Your kind words will do far more good to your child than botched routines will do harm.

Quit peering over the fence and focus on your own house. Within each home, your child should know what to expect and what comes next in her everyday activities. Create a routine. If you allow your child to eat breakfast while watching TV sometimes, but randomly demand her to eat at the table, it becomes confusing and unsettling. When chaos is the norm, your child will lose the confidence to carry out her activities. Be aware of activities in your home where routine can be established and then be consistently implemented.

Although the routines don't need to be identical, don't disregard your ex's suggestions. Be open to communication with your ex regarding your child's routines. When it comes to problem areas with your child, all suggestions should be welcome. If your ex has discovered a routine that eases your daughter to bed, then it should be considered, gratefully. The point is to do what's best for your child in your own home, and sometimes that means incorporating suggestions from others. Leave micromanaging out of the visitation routine, which leaves room to discuss the larger issues when necessary.

Divorced Situation 10

VISITATION: Never Change the Schedule, Except...

Does your child's tantrums give cause to change the schedule? Does your "night out" interfere with her visitation? How quick are you to suggest that your ex's visit be scrapped or switched? Don't minimize the importance of the schedule. Once the schedule has been established, stick to it.

The Old Way

"Whaaaaaaa!" wails your young child, as her fists are flailing and her heels are hitting the ground. As her rescuing mother, you plead to your ex, "***Ohhhh***, but she doesn't want to go today!! Just look at her crying. It wouldn't hurt for her to stay home with me tonight. Come here, honey, it's going to be alright."

or

"[Eyes rolling. Deep sighs. Don't-talk-to-me expression.]" says your teenager as your ex is waiting in the car. Ever the protecting mother, you implore to your ex, "You have no idea the stress she is under: school, girlfriends, boyfriends! She really just needs to stay home tonight. Come here, honey, it's going to be alright."

Thank goodness you were there! The ever-knowing, ever-caring, ever-superior parent has once again saved her child from the clutches of visitation. Peace has been restored to your child and her life can continue uninterrupted. You smile at your triumph.

Or perhaps you're the culprit to the failed visitation. Have you ever changed the schedule because you wanted to go see a movie instead of having your visitation? What about when your college roommate flew in to celebrate her birthday? Surely that is cause for changing the visitation schedule!

Things come up. Schedules change. Everyone is OK with the change. So, what's the big deal anyway?

> ♡
> *By honoring the visitation schedule,*
> *you show your child that you value her*
> *relationship with both of her parents.*

The Pro ♥ Child Way

The big deal is your child. The visitation schedule should never change. Your child has scheduled plans to be with you. You have scheduled plans to be with her. Nothing should interfere with that schedule. Not her bad mood. Not her newly rescheduled ballet class. Not your hot date. Not your ex's hot date. Nothing interferes with the schedule.

Your child's moods should never affect the visitation schedule. **Never.** Your child should learn right away that she cannot manipulate the visitation schedule through her moods. It is up to you and your ex to create an environment that eases the visitation transition. If a tantrum still erupts, then continue the visitation as planned. Your child should hear you exclaim, "Bye honey!" Once you give in to one episode, the never-ending spiral begins. Before you know it, your child will be in full control of the visitation schedule. As her parents, trust in the schedule that you arranged and implement it. Keep in mind that your child's time with her other parent isn't punishment: it is a valuable part of her life. You're not being horrible by making her stick to the schedule, you're being a loving parent who can see beyond a tantrum.

What about that rescheduled ballet class? Well, what about it? Why would that change the visitation? If it's your ex's Friday night, it looks like your ex is now the taxi driver to ballet. The schedule goes unchanged – just be sure to tell him right away.

Just as your child's moods shouldn't affect the schedule, so shouldn't your moods. The visitation schedule is designed so that every Friday night you are responsible for your daughter. Don't make other plans. You already have plans with your child. When an unavoidable event does arise, get a babysitter. Your child is still your responsibility. The visitation schedule stands. By honoring the schedule, you show your child that you value her relationship with both of her parents. Your child learns that visitation is something that can be counted on and not manipulated by her or you or her other parent. This is critical in establishing a secure child – *especially* in the beginning of your divorce. Perhaps after several years, flexibility will be appropriate, but when in doubt, stick to the schedule.

Of course there will be times when a change in schedule is unavoidable. Give plenty of notice and reschedule. After communicating with your ex, explain the change to your child. Tell her that you and Dad have already discussed it, and tell her the age-appropriate reason. Children are reasonable when their parents are reasonable. If you have maintained visitation consistency, your child will understand.

Cherish the time that you get to spend with your child. Let your child cherish the time that she gets to spend with her dad. Don't interrupt the visitation schedule. Through consistency and your Pro♥Child attitude, the visitation bumps will smooth.

The "sick" factor: If your child is truly sick with a high fever, nausea, or other debilitating ailment, then she should be where she is most comfortable and receive the best care, regardless of the visitation schedule. But remember to include your child in this decision. This is one area when she does get a choice. Your child shouldn't feel punished just because she was sick – if she still wants to go to Dad's, then she should go. If she wants to stay with you when she's very sick, then she should stay. And she needs to know that both of her parents support her, without gloat or guilt.

Divorced Situation ▌▌

VISITATION: Your Child's Activities Continue, Regardless of Visitation

The phone clicks off and you're left staring at the receiver. Your ex called to tell you about your child's schedule during **your** visitation period. You were hoping for some quiet time with your child, and now you learn that her events will be interfering. How do you respond? Recognize that your child has a life. Willingly share in your child's activities so that you can be involved in **her** life.

The *Old* Way

It's finally your time with your child. Friday night and all-day Saturday: that's the schedule. But, as it's turning out, not only do you get your child, but also your child's softball game **and** her friend's birthday party. Wait a minute. The divorce agreement clearly states that Friday and Saturday is with you, and you're seeing very little "with you" time happening in the next 24 hours.

Visitation isn't supposed to be this way. This is your time, and you're going to demand it. Forget the softball game – besides, you wanted her to go out for soccer, **not** softball. And forget the birthday party – you know it's for a "friend" of your ex! There's no way that your time is being interrupted for your child to go to **that!** This is your visitation time. You get to decide **if** and **what** your child does on **your** time. This time, your child is spending time with **you.**

♡ *Instead of bemoaning your child's activities, be glad that she is involved, and cheerfully support her.*

28

The *Pro♥Child* Way

Your child's life goes on: divorce or no divorce. After-school activities, sports, and friends don't go away just because her parents got divorced. Whether your child is at your house or at Dad's house, her life should go on.

Face it: time is limited for school-age children. When you factor in homework, dinner, and sleep, it doesn't leave much time for haircuts, playing, and activities. At some point, all parents feel the squeeze of their child's activities. Being divorced may just accentuate it. As much as you may want to characterize visitation as "your" time, it isn't. It is, above all, "your child's" time. If you've fostered security in your child, then she will know that your love can absorb a few missed hours. Instead of bemoaning your child's activities, be glad that she is involved, and cheerfully support her. Be involved and interested, but don't interrupt your child's life. Recognize that it is your job, as a parent, to guide your child through all of these experiences. Sure, you may feel like a taxi, but use what time you have, and cherish it.

Know that activities pop up, so regularly consult with your ex. New plans, for which you should be aware, are bound to come up. Last month, your child's schedule may have looked clear, but that was before tryouts were announced and the party invitation was received. Sure, your ex shouldn't make plans on "your time" without consulting you, but usually it's your child that is busy making plans. You shouldn't prohibit your child from making plans, but as the parent, you can set the guidelines.

Of course you can say "no" to your child's disrupting activity, but unless a compelling reason is evident to you **and** your child, don't arbitrarily deny her activities. Instead, create guidelines for her to navigate within. If her event is a sporting event, then the rule could be that you get to observe it. If her event is time with friends, then the rule could be that you first must visit their home. You are the parent; be one by staying involved.

Recognize that there is a difference between your child's activities and your ex's activities for your child. If your ex is arranging interruptions to your visitation, then address that with your ex. Perhaps you don't mind taking your child for her haircut, or perhaps you do. Regardless, these appointment-based plans should be discussed with you prior to being made. The best way to avoid being "set-up" is to lay the ground rules with your ex. "Please consult with me before making any plans for our child during my visitation time. I wouldn't want to disappoint our child because the plans conflict with our other plans. Let me know if any appointments need to be made, and I'll make them directly." Again, just to be sure that there are no surprises, call your ex the day or two before visitation to check your child's schedule.

Don't make your child pay the price for your divorce. Her plans and activities shouldn't have to change just because her parents aren't together. What was norm prior to the divorce should be norm afterwards, regardless of whose time it falls under.

Divorced Situation **12**

HOLIDAYS: Setting the Holiday Schedule

For divorced parents, setting the holiday schedule can be fraught with conflict and high emotions. In the confrontational arena of formulating custody arrangements, it is easy for the focus to shift away from the child's best interest and move towards a competition between the opposing parents. In response to wanting to end the conflict, the compromising old way of "every-other" results. The typical every-other approach to dividing up holidays may be a shortcut for avoiding initial conflict, but the long-term effects can be unsettling for your child. Instead, lay a secure foundation by adopting the designated holiday schedule. Once the schedule is set, turn your attention to your child and the holidays. Strive to create holidays that are filled with thoughts of yummy food, good times, and tradition.

The *Old* Way

If it's an even number year, then that must mean that your child will be forced to be with her dad for Christmas. The good news is that at least this year, you get to spend Thanksgiving with your child. Of course, last year your child had to suffer through Thanksgiving with her dad's family – **that** didn't go well. They made spaghetti. Spaghetti! This year, since it's your turn, you'll be making that turkey. Turkey, and maybe a ham, and stuffing, and pumpkin pie from a fresh pumpkin. You'll show her what a **real** Thanksgiving looks like. Would it be going too far to wear Pilgrim and Indian costumes? That would be a cool picture for her to show her dad.

Thanksgiving will be better this year – for her and you.

Last year was really depressing without her. Of course, Christmas will be even worse this year. She really loves all of her cousins and the hubbub of the large family Christmas morning. This year, it will just be her and her dad. That's going to stink. Last year, when he was alone, he traveled to his family's house. But this year, it's just too expensive for them both to travel. I guess it's going to stink for him too. Oh well, that's divorce.

As you're mulling over the year's upcoming holidays, trying to stomach the disappointments and making glorious plans for the shared dates, your heart is aching. No matter what year it is – odd or even – something is going to suck. Holidays used to be such a highlight. Those years are over.

♡ *Foster that sense of tradition, continuity, and security by adopting the designated holiday schedule.*

The *Pro ♥ Child* Way

So, if the "every-other" solution to divvying-up holidays is out, what is the solution? The solution is to designate each specific holiday with a specific parent, and stick to that schedule year after year. New Years is spent with Dad, every year. Easter is spent with Mom, every year. Thanksgiving is spent with Dad, every year. You get the idea.

Your protesting is heard loud and clear: it is certainly easier (and less confrontational) for you to create the typical "every-other" approach. But remember, the point isn't for it to be easy for you; the point is for it to be the best for your child. The "every-other" holiday schedule doesn't work. "Every-other" is confusing for all, and it hampers establishing tradition, routine, and security for your child. The pains of determining the holiday schedule are worth the benefits that they will bring year after year.

When deciding the schedule, it is important to consider what is best and most comforting for your child. Does your child look forward to Dad's backyard firework display on the Fourth of July? Then perhaps that summertime holiday should be spent with Dad. Is Christmas Day special because of Mom's traditions and cooking? Then Christmas should be with Mom. This isn't about what you want. This isn't about getting "your fair share." This isn't about your winning or losing. This is only about making your child's holidays the best they can be.

But what if one parent took the lead at all holidays? If both parents agree, there is nothing wrong with your child spending every holiday with the one parent. However, it is wrong for you and your child to be inconsiderate and not remember the other parent on holidays. You want your child to grow up knowing that she is loved and thought of by both parents. In turn, a happy child will love and think of her parents. Days before the holiday, have your child prepare something for her other parent: a card, a drawing, or a poem. On holidays, take the lead and provide guidance by having your child call the other parent first thing in the morning and again in the evening to share the day's events. Your child's remembering the other parent should become part of that holiday's tradition.

But what if both parents were actively involved in all holidays? If both parents continue to stay involved in each holiday, then that is great for your child! There is nothing wrong with trick-or-treating at both houses, or Easter morning at one house followed by an egg hunt at the other. *Important warning: be sure that this "dual parents holiday" adds to the celebration, not to the burden.* If it disrupts your child's day, then it isn't a positive addition. The key is to celebrate the holiday consistently, year after year. The goal is for your child to grow up surrounded in happy holiday traditions.

If the "dual parents holiday" simply isn't an option, then roll up your sleeves – this is when it gets difficult to divvy-up the holidays, but divvy you must do. Each parent should create a full list of the holidays. Thinking of your child's experience at each holiday, number them according to your child's involvement with you during that holiday. Tackle the "big ones" last and start with the easier holidays. Keep in mind that some holidays are a natural fit: an outsider would recognize that your ex's celebrating Irish family would offer your child a more enriching St. Paddy's Day than your non-Irish family. Use the "outsider's perspective" to check your reality. Hopefully you and your ex can agree on where your child should spend each holiday, but you may have to compromise. Remember: The compromise isn't to switch to an every-other schedule. Designate.

Most importantly, the goal is to create wonderful holidays for your child – holidays that are full of tradition and love. Designating holidays allows for you and your child to repeat traditions every year. (And not comparing it to the other parent's traditions.) Even seemingly silly events like your child creating place-cards for the dinner table evolve into concrete traditions that help define that holiday. Foster that sense of tradition, continuity, and security by adopting the designated holiday schedule.

A terrific effect of this schedule is that both parents seem to put more effort into creating wonderful holidays. Former lack-luster holidays develop into fun new celebrations. Your child benefits from this extra effort, making the holidays wonderful family times for all.

Divorced Situation 13

HOLIDAYS: Gift Giving

Every month brings a different holiday. Every holiday brings up the issue of "gifts." When you are divorced, gift-giving holidays can be tricky. How do you handle your child's gift that is intended for your ex? As much as you may want to avoid the whole gift-giving/ex routine, your child will not. So, that leaves you with questions: What does your child give to her other parent? Are you going to make your ex's gift all about you or all about your child? The choice is yours, but the consequence is your child's. Teach your child about the spirit of giving.

The *Old* Way

"What are we getting Dad?" your child inquires. When it comes to gift-giving holidays and presents for your ex, you can be thrown into two tempting directions. You pause to answer … on the one hand, why should you spend time and money on a gift for your ex? "C'mon," you sneer, "that jerk? I'm not buying him a darn thing." You're not going to give him the time of day, let alone a present, and you certainly aren't going to spend a dime. Gift-giving holiday? Baaaah! The day you got divorced is the day the presents stopped. If your ex thinks it's a good idea to receive a present from his child, then he can take her shopping for it. Your ex will most definitely not be getting any presents from you!

But … on the other hand, now that you think about it, a gift might not be such a bad idea – especially a gift that is dripping in revenge and innuendoes. Spoiled chocolates, dead flowers, a big box of nothing, a picture of you and your child? Why not? Sounds like the perfect gift for such a louse. Just thinking about it brings a Grinch-inspired smirk to your face. You perk up when you think of each gift-giving holiday as a new opportunity for revenge. Besides, is he getting anything for you?

Through all of this thought, preparation, and activity, your child learns the joy in giving to others.

The *Pro* ♥ *Child* Way

It's not about you! It's not your gift for your ex; it's not his gift for you. Exes don't buy each other gifts. Children buy their parents gifts, and this is your child's gift for her dad. This is about your child and fostering a better relationship between her and her dad.

When it comes to divorce, your child's gift-giving shouldn't change at all. A child should naturally want to give her parents something to mark a special occasion. That shouldn't change just because her parents are divorced. Your child should give, as well as receive, and your only role is to help her. Smaller children need more guidance, but all children need your support.

Have your child prepare for a holiday by thinking of her dad and his family. What would she like to give them? Has she thought of any ideas already? We all treasure the gifts that our children make for us, so encourage special handmade items. A trip to the craft store can offer many inexpensive options. Does your child's dad live far away? Then how about some plain envelopes adorned with crayons and stickers, addressed back to her? Or turn the rock collection into paperweights painted with love. Whatever the gift, don't let a holiday pass without some special gift from your child.

Holidays give us an excuse to do something out of the ordinary. It isn't just any Tuesday – it's Groundhog Day! Why spend another day doing the same old, same old, when you can make it special. Cookies, drawings, cards, or crafts can all distinguish a holiday. Have fun working on these projects together, talking about the holiday and how much Dad will love his gift.

When occasions call for a bought gift, make a day out of going with your child to find that special gift. Is she looking for a tie? Avoid the rush in, rush out, grab any tie that you see. Instead, take time with your child to look at a selection. Which tie does she think Dad will like best? Make sure she is happy with the choice. After all, it is her gift. Here's a tip: consider shopping at theme or cartoon character stores. Your child may be too young to decide between a sweatshirt or gloves, but she can definitely decide on her favorite character that adorns the various clothes. These gifts keep the present geared towards her, and away from any personalized gesture from her divorced parents.

Don't forget the wrapping paper. Wrapping paper should be part of your child's creation. Whether it's for a birthday, Valentine's Day, or Christmas, personalized paper is the finishing touch on her special gift. Praise creativity, not neatness!

Through all of this thought, preparation, and activity, your child learns the joy in giving to others. Your child learns that it is OK for her to think of, talk about, and make plans involving her dad. It is so important for you to support the relationships that are important to her. One way to show this is by embracing gift-giving holidays.

Divorced Situation **14**

HOLIDAYS: Phone Calls

Like most days, your child is with one parent and away from the other. But this isn't just any day. This is a holiday. On this day, everything is extra special, including your love for your child. Your child needs to hear holiday wishes from both parents. Don't think of your phone call as an interruption but as welcome nourishment to your child's heart. When calling your child, don't focus on the predictable ex-in-law grief. Focus instead on sharing this special day with your child.

The *Old* Way

On the morning of the holiday, you wake up and start thinking. Through your fog, you remember that your child isn't with you to celebrate, she is with your ex. And then in horror, it hits you: she is visiting the relatives. The ex relatives. The ex in-laws. Your stomach starts turning in knots as you imagine all of those exes in one place. That setting is ripe for a bash fest on you. You can almost hear their buzzing as you duck your head back under the covers. Oh, the things they must be saying about you! Never have you been so glad to be so far away.

Call your child? There? You don't think so. It's bad enough dealing with your ex. It's absolutely distressing dealing with his family. No way. **No way!** Besides, if you were crazy enough to call, your ex in-law would answer and wouldn't let you speak to your child anyway. They would start ranting at you. They could care less about your side of the story. All they care about is how rotten you are, and there is no way you're going to give them a chance to tell you their opinion. In the end, you would probably get hung-up on. Seriously, not worth the call.

Making contact with your child on the holiday isn't worth the abuse that you will get from the ex in-laws. The holiday will be over soon enough. Besides, your child knows that you love her and that you're thinking of her. You'll catch up when she returns. You groan and roll back under the covers.

♡ *Hearing that she is remembered and cared for is priceless for your child.*

The *Pro ♥ Child* **Way**

As you dial the phone, trying to reach your child at her grandparents' house during the holidays, remember: you're doing this for your child. Your ex's mother doesn't have to be nice to you. Your ex's sister can hiss when she hears your voice. Ignore their tone. Remember that you and your ex have discussed your call; wish the in-laws a happy holiday, and ask to speak to your child.

Your child needs to hear your voice when she is away from you on a holiday. She needs to hear you say, "I love you! And Happy Thanksgiving!" She needs to hear that you are thinking of her and wishing her a great day. She needs to tell you of her day and activities. She may just need to tell you a joke. Don't let your fear of calling get in the way of this phone call.

Prior to the holiday, you and your ex should talk about appropriate times to call and should agree that the phone call is an important part of the day's events. Hopefully, your ex will be expecting your call on the holiday and answer the phone. More than likely, however, it will be his family that picks up the phone. Divorces have a damaging effect on both extended families, and often, exchanges with family members are not pleasant. No matter what the response or tone is on the other side, remember to focus on one thing: talking to your child. Don't become involved in a conversation or argument with your ex's family. Simply ignore any comments and ask to speak to your child. If they persist, repeat, "*[Insert ex's name]* knows I'm calling, and I just called to wish [insert child's name] a Merry Christmas and to speak to her, is she there?" Make sure that you stay calm and true to your goal. Remember that you can't control your in-laws. You can't make them hand over the phone. If they refuse, stay polite while briefly stating your disappointment, then hang up. Take heart that over time, this will get easier. This also gets easier once your child has her own cell phone!

Once your child gets on the phone, put all negative emotions aside and focus on a lovely talk with your child. Making a phone call to your ex in-laws is hard. Getting to talk to your child is your reward. Hearing that she is remembered and cared for is priceless for your child.

Is your child with you for the holiday? If so, then encourage your child's communication with her other parent. It is so important for your child to have a touch point with both of her parents on a holiday: a morning phone call to wish her dad a "Merry Christmas" and an evening talk to sum up the day's events.

When you and your child are at your family's house for the holidays, be considerate to your child's dad and expect his call. Don't let his call create confrontation with your family. Tell your family that he will be calling, so that they can let you answer the phone if needed. "*[Child's name] is looking forward to her dad calling today, so be sure to listen for the phone so we don't miss the call!*" Your child understands insincerity. Avoid it.

Remember that the point of this call isn't to interrupt your child's holiday, but to put a smile on her face. With your pre-planning, this phone call "hello" can become a welcome addition to your child's holiday tradition.

Divorced Situation 15

HOLIDAYS: Dealing with Your Own Emotions When Your Child Is Away

The holiday is upon you and your child will be spending it with your ex. After all of the preparations are made and the last goodbyes are waved, you are left with you. For a parent who is alone for a holiday, there is little consolation in knowing that the best arrangements were made. But as the saying goes: "When life hands you lemons…." As the holiday approaches, make plans for yourself. Not only will this benefit you, but also your child. Your child always benefits by knowing that you're OK too. So as the childless holiday approaches, which way will you choose: the Old Way of loneliness and avoidance or the Pro♥Child way of celebration?

The *Old* Way

Your child is scheduled to be with your ex for the upcoming holiday. You get depressed just thinking about it. It's going to suck. You figure, why decorate or celebrate at all? Your child won't be here anyway, what's the point?

As the holiday draws nearer, the stores fill with decorations, while your house fills with loneliness. The only indication of the approaching holiday is the seasonal decoration that your child made in school. It hangs, out of context, on the refrigerator door. Its presence only reminds you of how lonely you are going to be.

You get more depressed with each passing day. You wonder how you'll ever make it through another holiday without your child. Without your child there to celebrate, there simply isn't a point to any of the hoopla.

As your child leaves for her holiday, you fight back the tears, leaving a blank stare on your face. Your parting gift to your child is your blanket of sadness. A heavy weight that travels with her. You're too depressed to care.

♥
Seeing you happy and content with the holiday arrangements allows your child to enjoy herself while with Dad.

The Pro ♥ Child Way

Holidays without your child are hard. Certainly, one of the worst aspects of divorce is not being able to spend every holiday with your child. But the holiday will arrive, whether you are with or without your child. So prepare for it and make your own traditions. Doing this is good for you and good for your child.

First off, take the decorations out of storage and have your child help you decorate the house. She may not be there for Thanksgiving Day, but that doesn't mean you should skip on the season. Decorating for a holiday is great fun and a terrific opportunity to create tradition with your child. There are so many activities, decorations, and foods that you and your child can create. It would be a shame to give it all up, just because you won't be together for the actual holiday. Your child doesn't have to give up making handprint turkey place-cards just because she isn't having dinner with you. Ask your ex if it would be OK if some of the decorations traveled with your child. The place-cards can just as easily include the names of those celebrating with her. Besides, it gives your child a part in decorating for her holiday as well.

Have a "pre-holiday" event with your child. Is the upcoming holiday Halloween? Then why not have your own Halloween party with decorated cupcakes, costumes, spooky games, and stories? If Easter is the holiday that will be spent with Dad, then consider hosting a pre-Easter egg-making party and hunt. If Thanksgiving is the date, then cook a full-blown dinner that previous Sunday and be thankful. Your goal is not to "out-do" Dad's celebration, but to create your own happy day. Even if it is just the two of you, these pre-holiday celebrations will become an important part of each holiday.

Consider your child's feelings. If you do not decorate or celebrate a holiday, your child will be sad for you. Wouldn't you be sad to know that your loved one wasn't going to celebrate a holiday? Indeed, it would be hard for you to be happy on that day, knowing that your favorite person was spending it depressed. Your child would react in the same way. Seeing you happy and content with the holiday arrangements allows her to enjoy herself with Dad. Give your child that gift.

Once your child has left for her visit, go ahead and cry all you need to. At some point, the tears will be over and you'll need to get on with life. Foresee a rough holiday and make other plans. Don't sit and eat leftover spaghetti on Thanksgiving; don't sleep through Christmas Day. There are so many events in which you could get involved. Spend the day with other family or friends, volunteer to help others, or spend the day at the spa. Just plan something and make that your new tradition.

Look forward to the day's phone call when you and your child can share the holiday's events. In addition to hearing about her holiday, be sure to tell her about your great day.

Finally, take comfort in knowing that your child is with her dad who loves her, and that she is getting to spend the day with him. Congratulate yourself on helping your child have a great holiday experience, with or without you.

SECTION 2

PARENTS TOGETHER:
Out and About with Your Child
and Your Ex

A Few Words About "Parents Together"

Given the choice, would you choose to spend countless days with your ex? Of course not. That is why your ex is your ex. The choice has already been made: it is called "divorce." When you say that you are "divorced," people automatically assume that spending time with your ex is not your ideal day. This is most likely the reason why divorced couples who don't share a child part ways for good. People get it. Divorced couples aren't the best playmates at a social gathering. Outsiders don't need a flow-chart, PowerPoint demonstration, or dissertation. They get it. Everyone gets it. Divorced couples are generally divorced because they didn't enjoy each other's company.

But here you are, divorced with a shared child. You are a divorced parent and the world "gets it." The world realizes that divorced parents, like divorced couples, would rather not spend any moments together. Again, the world doesn't need you to yell it from a blow-horn. It's kind of understood that there were past issues and problems between the couple that led to the divorce. People even assume that at least one within the couple was a jerk. A jerk? Shocking. Hence: divorced. Public events aren't your opportunity to share this tedious information. They already know. And so does your child.

Get over yourself. Get over the pre-divorce stuff. Move on. Here you are *now.* How are you going to act *now*? For better or worse (don't you hate that phrase?), your divorce is decided and what you have in your control is how you choose to act *now.* Every day, every situation, every phone call: you have the choice as to how you're going to act with your child's other parent. With the whole world assuming the animosity between the divorce couple, you have your work cut out for you. It is up to *you* to choose to stop showing your child the anger, hate, and stress of a divorced marriage and instead show her the love that two parents have for their very special child.

Not only should you encourage moments where you and your ex are together with your child, but also you should be smiling throughout the event. This is why it is called "Parents Together." As Parents Together you choose to silence the world (and your ego) and tune into your heart and your child's needs. Your child needs both parents to love, support, and guide her. Put on the blinders, and even a muzzle if you have to, but stay focused on your child and be nice to your ex. Choose to show your child that her two parents can finally focus on her. With every opportunity, choose to parent the Pro♡Child Way. With every visitation exchange, choose. With every phone call, choose. With every event where you know your child will see you interacting with her other parent, choose to parent the Pro♡Child Way. It only takes one to make a significant impact on the divorced-parenting tone. It only takes you to choose it to be so. Choose carefully – your child is watching. Choose to tend to her heart and spirit.

♡
It only takes one to make a significant impact on the divorced-parenting tone. It only takes you to choose it to be so. Choose carefully – your child is watching.

Divorced Situation **16**

PARENTS TOGETHER: Plan for It Now and Do It

Here is a fact: throughout your child's life, you and your ex will be together in the same room. Whether you encourage this joint participation or whether you try to avoid it, it will happen again and again. You can't control that. What you can control is you. When you and your ex are together, will you resist and cause tension in front of your child, or will you be Parents Together?

The *Old* Way

Your ex and you are forced to be in the same room together. He is being rude and condescending to you. You are angry and miserable to him. Everyone around you is uncomfortable, and the tension in the air is thick. And why should it be any other way? Your divorce was messy. He doesn't like you, and you certainly don't like him.

Instead of focusing on your child's event, you are preoccupied trying to cope with your ex's presence. All of your attention is on your ex: where he goes, what he does, who he talks to. Everyone around you becomes aware that they are in the presence of a warring couple. You make excuses for both of your behaviors. All of the attention is on two divorced people. By the end of the event, you're stressed and have a headache.

Your child had her own expectations of the day: a great event where she would be the center of attention. And the best part would be the two most important people in her world, her mom and dad, would be there to share it with her. Imagine her disappointment. She hopes that another event never arises where her parents will have to be together with her again. Instead of looking forward to birthdays, graduations, and her wedding, she is already learning that her "non-divorced friends" will have wonderful events, while she will have events to avoid. And this is all because you and your ex can't get over your divorce and focus on your child. At the end of the day, after witnessing your theatrics, she is crushed.

♡
*Let her know that you will both
always be there to support, help,
and celebrate with her,
free of conflict or tension.*

Parents Together: Plan for It Now and Do It

The *Pro❤Child* Way

The reason that you and your ex are forced into the same room is because of your child. Being a parent is forever, so being in the same room with your ex is something that you need to get used to.

As a child, the happiest moments should be the times that the child, her mom, and her dad are together. This should not change just because her parents aren't married. There will be times, scattered throughout your child's life, that the whole family should be together. Your child should be able to make plans for happy days when both of her parents are present. Don't rob your child of these nurturing experiences. You may be divorced, but you are still parents. And parents do things with their children, together.

In any circumstance where your child is also present, the reason as to why the two of you need to be beyond cordial should be obvious. Your child needs to see that the two most important people in her life like each other. Yes, like each other.

Discuss the important day or event with your child, mentioning her dad's inclusion in a positive way. Assure your child that you are both looking forward to spending the day with her. Let her know that you will both always be there to support, help, and celebrate with her, free of conflict or tension.

You both should help with the planning and the day's events. You both should be next to your child at the event. You both should ask questions and be concerned for your daughter's happiness and well-being. You both should thank guests for coming. And, you should make sure that pictures include all of the people who are important to her. Commit to being "Parents Together" on this day and throughout her life.

Divorced Situation **17**

PARENTS TOGETHER: The Birthday Party

The birthday party – there are two ways of looking at it: from the perspective of a divorced parent or from your child's perspective. The one way is sure to be filled with tension, bitterness, and accusations. The other way will be bursting with laughter and balloons. Which type of birthday will you choose for your child?

The *Old* Way

It's your child's birthday and that can mean only one thing: an ex disaster. No way are you going to spend your child's birthday with your ex. A stressed-out day fighting with your ex is not the type of birthday party that you had in mind. It's hard enough decorating, corralling a pack of kids, distributing party favors, keeping track of gifts, and serving cake. You *really* can't handle your ex's judging presence on top of all of that!

So you rationalize that excluding your ex from your child's birthday is the best thing. Everyone would agree that it would be better if your ex stayed far away, right? So, you start to plan a grand birthday party: one that includes your friends and your family. If your ex wants to celebrate, fine; he can arrange his own party. (It had just not be better than your party!) Come on, you're divorced! It would be so awkward. "Happy Birthday!" just isn't convincing when you're gritting your teeth. Certainly nobody would expect that the two of you would be at the same birthday party.

♡ *During any moments of tension, look at your child and remind yourself of the wonderful reason that you are there.*

The *Pro ♥ Child* Way

Well, almost no one would expect that two divorced parents would be at their child's birthday party … except maybe your child. Let's get something clear, right off the bat: this is your child's birthday party. Not yours. Not your ex's. It is her party, with her friends and her family. You are her family. Her other parent is her family. At your child's birthday party, she should see not just you, but also her dad celebrating the day of her birth. Of course your ex should be a vital part of your child's birthday. Who else has more to celebrate than the two people that created her? Celebrating a birthday is so important. Creating a wonderful birthday celebration is a joyful obligation for parents. You and your ex are her parents. Being divorced should have no impact on your child's day.

You're right, a stressed-out day, fighting with your ex is not the type of birthday party for your child. Your child does deserve better. But the answer isn't to have two separate parties. The answer is for you to be nice. Impossible, you say? With the right planning and attitude, it is possible.

Start planning your child's birthday by sizing up the situation: the date, the time of year, age and number of guests, your child's wishes, and also the current state of your relationship with your ex. As with all issues regarding your divorce, the more time has passed, the easier it will be. But in the beginning, your child's birthday party requires careful planning to avoid any scenes between you and your ex. Communicate often with your ex, to confirm all particulars.

On what day of the week does your child's birthday fall? Will you be able to celebrate it on the birth date or does it have to be celebrated on the weekend? Does it land on "Dad's day" or "Mom's day"? If it is "Dad's day," does he still want you to plan the event or is he assuming that it is his responsibility? It's time for a phone call, text, or email to your ex. During this call be sure to establish the date of celebration, the primary planner, and confirm that you both will be there. This is not an opportunity for you to talk about or respond to any issues involving your marriage or divorce. Stay focused and positive.

Now that you are assured of the date, you can worry about planning the event. Location is usually the trickiest part of planning a birthday. In selecting a site, you should have one focus: neutral territory. Avoid your ex coming to an event at your house. It has too high a disaster potential. And you shouldn't be keen on going to his house for the same reasons. Hold the party at a location that is neutral: the playground, pool, or local pizza shop are some suggestions. You want the location to be a place that will be remembered fondly as "her birthday spot," not the scene of tension between you and your ex. Find a place that is perfect for young guests and perfect for adults who need more space. Down the road, as your relationship with your ex matures, the location of her parties can be determined by the theme, but in the beginning, careful location planning helps to lessen the stress between two newly divorced parents.

Once you have the location secured, you can plan the birthday activities. Homespun games, decorations, and birthday cake are benign issues in regards to your ex. However, if you are envisioning a rented moon bounce, a hired clown, and pony rides, the expense may be of concern to your ex. Know your budget. What, if anything, is your ex willing to contribute? Do not plan to spend his money unless he has agreed. This is not a "blank check" opportunity to test your ex's love for his child. Think back to your married years: How were birthdays handled then? If your ex thought homespun birthdays were best back then, chances are neither his attitude nor his wallet have changed. Don't assume that he will pay for all the incidentals. Don't assume that he will evenly share the expense. The only thing that you can assume is that you will be financially responsible for the event. If you are not able to afford the entire bill, then don't plan an expensive party. Plan the party that you can afford. If he is able to contribute to the expenses, then it will be a surprise benefit to your checkbook. At all times, be considerate of both of your financial situations when planning events. It's time for another phone call to your ex. Which scenario fits the party that you are envisioning?

The party that doesn't require his financial participation:

"I thought a party at the playground pavilion would be best. The preschoolers will love being able to run around and play. I can make the cake and bring the decorations. I'll buy a book for each child to take home, which I can pay for out of her child support. Sound good?"

or

The party that requires his financial participation:

"This has been such a great school year for our child. Her whole class is working together as a team and she is having a hard time excluding anyone. I think this year we should have a larger party where all her classmates can be included. I was thinking a carnival-type party where we can have games, crafts, the sprinkler running, and a rented moon bounce. Do you think we can swing that? The moon bounce is about $300 for the day, and I figure the crafts, prizes for the games, and food will be another $100. I can use $100 from her child support, but that leaves $300. Would you be able to contribute $150 if we split the remainder? Can you come up with a game idea and be in charge of that booth? I'll be sure to tell our child that this is an extra-special birthday party for just this year."

Once the date, the location, and the budget are determined, all that remains is getting ready for the big day. If invitations are being sent, be sure to have your child send one to you and one to her dad. She can include a special message or drawing in these VIP invitations. As the day approaches, frequently mention how both you and Dad are looking forward to her special birthday. Not only does that get her excited, but it also reinforces positive thoughts in your mind too.

Your child's excitement should be contagious and propel you through a wonderful birthday. Start the day with a smile and continue it through the whole day. During any moments of tension, look at your child and remind yourself of the wonderful reason that you are there. Stick to your plan of being Parents Together, and you will be able to create happy birthday memories and picture-perfect occasions.

Divorced Situation 18

PARENTS TOGETHER: Your Child's Extracurricular Activities

If you're lucky, your child will be involved in many extracurricular activities. These are precious moments where you can enthusiastically support and celebrate your child's efforts. But how does your reaction change when your ex is also there? If your child's lucky, she will have both of her parents rooting and cheering her on together.

The Old Way

It's your child's soccer game. For you, it's another grueling event because you know your ex will also be attending. You have one goal in mind: to avoid your ex at all costs. You can't stop him from coming, but you sure can make it real uncomfortable for him. He needs a seat? Tough, he should have gotten there earlier like you did. He doesn't know that he's standing next to the coach? Typical, just goes to show that he is so out of touch. He thinks he can cheer and clap just to prove a point to you? Well, you can cheer and clap louder. You look around and hope that everyone else is noticing what a jerk he is.

You might as well be holding a sign over your head that says, "Divorced Parent." All those around you can clearly see that you are the "Divorced Mom" and that man over there, cheering for the same child, is the "Divorced Dad." The child is also easy to spot. She is the one that doesn't know where to look when she scores a goal: the right or left, Mom or Dad. She is embarrassed by her parents' cheering competition and wishes she could have normal parents like the other kids. Maybe, she thinks, it would be better if they didn't show up at all.

Your child needs to see both of her parents involved, interested, and participating in her activities.

The *Pro ♥ Child* Way

There is nothing better than rallying behind your child's extracurricular activities. What a thrill for your child to make that hoop shot or perfect dismount, then turn around to see her parents cheering for her. Come on, you and her dad are on the same team! That's your child out there, doing a great job. You and your ex should be proud of her and proud to be her parents, together. What does "divorced" have to do with anything?

You and your ex should sit together, cheer together, and give each other high-fives when your child succeeds. Is it the big dance recital? Then make sure he has a ticket and save him a seat. Is it the important away game? Then make sure he has directions. Is it yet another practice? Then make sure he gets an opportunity to be there to see her effort. If the responsibility falls on your shoulders to get your ex involved in your child's activities, then do it. Your child needs to see both of her parents involved, interested, and participating in her activities. When both of you are able to make it to an activity, be there as "Parents Together."

The sign above your heads should exclaim, "Parents who are proud of their child." In public, don't act-up; act like parents. After all, that's what you are and that is what your child needs.

Divorced Situation 19

PARENTS TOGETHER:
School Functions – Back-to-School Night

"Back-to-School Night" is a school-wide version of show-and-tell. It is your child's opportunity to show and tell about her accomplishments, projects, and classmates. But at this event, what do your actions show and tell? Do you tell two divorced parents, or are you a family that shows off together?

The *Old* Way

It's Back-to-School Night? "Just great," you sarcastically sigh. Another occasion that you'll have to suffer through with your ex. Well no more! The solution is at hand: you divide the event in half. The first half of the evening is your turn and the second half of the event will be your ex's turn. Yep, that's right. Your child can first show you her classroom, her seat, her books, her poem on the wall, and her favorite classroom activity. Then it's off to show you the way to the art room, the gym, the music room, the cafeteria, and the bathrooms. Once the whole school is covered once or twice at a jog, you can leave so that your ex can arrive.

Once your ex arrives, your child can show him the classroom, her seat, and her books. Forget the poem and her favorite classroom activity, time will be running out and Dad will still need to see the gym. He can't see it all? Too bad. At least you avoided each other and that is most important. Given the circumstances, you fit in what you could.

By being Parents Together,
you show her that she is important,
not the divorce.

The $Pro \heartsuit Child$ **Way**

When Back-to-School Night is split in two, what is usually a fun and proud night for a child turns into a burden. Your child becomes more worried about crossing between Mom's time and Dad's time, and less focused on showing off her accomplishments. The night is exhausting for your child, less than fulfilling for the parents, and the whole point of the evening is lost.

What can be more fun for your young child than for the whole family "gang" focusing on her at Back-to-School Night? Her mom, her dad, her siblings, her step-parents, her step-siblings – all there for her. For days, her classroom has prepared for the big night: cleaning up the desks, creating projects for display, and putting finishing touches on creative stories. She is proud of her work and anxious to show it off. There are teachers to meet and other kids to see. It's like a big, exciting party for your child where she is the star attraction. The more to share it with her, the merrier!

This is an event specifically designed for parents. As her parents, you should be there, together. Be sure that your ex has plenty of notice so that he can plan on attending. You should walk together, ooh and aah together, and greet the teachers together. There are usually parent sign-up sheets to register for conferences or participate in classroom parties. You and your ex should consider these together and sign up when appropriate.

You and your ex should have fun with your child and be glad that she is excited to show off her classroom activities. By being Parents Together, you show her that she is important, not the divorce.

Divorced Situation 20

PARENTS TOGETHER:
School Functions – Parent/Teacher Conferences

You open up your child's backpack and there it is: the parent/teacher conference announcement. So how are you going to approach this year's conference? In typical fashion, you could be the divorced parent that expects "divorced-parent' treatment from the teacher. Or, you could be the supportive parents that your child needs and show up as Parents Together.

The Old Way

The Old Way of the divorced-parent/teacher conference is so ingrained in the teacher's routine that it is shocking to a teacher when it is any other way. Separated parents equals separated conferences. The teacher meets with the mom at one time and the dad at a separate time. Through painful experience, the teacher has learned to avoid the scene between two feuding parents. She has enough to deal with, why would she want divorced parents in her classroom at the same time?

If a single meeting with both parents is unavoidable, the teacher comes armed with two copies of all reports and articles: one for the mom and one for the dad. She arranges the seating so that the parents are well separated. After all, the child's parents are divorced, these are necessary precautions to avoid conflict. The teacher's only goal is to get through the conference without any major incidences between the parents. She doesn't have to think hard to understand why the child acts the way she does at school.

♡
Your child can only benefit when her mom and dad are a cohesive unit, both actively participating in her school affairs.

The *Pro ♥ Child* Way

Stop and think about it: why does being divorced have any impact on how your child's teacher should relate to you? It doesn't. Just because you and your child's dad are divorced, don't expect that special accommodations should be made for you. Why should your child's teacher have to do extra work and spend extra time, just because you two are divorced? We are talking about the same child here, right?

Parent/teacher conferences happen. Expect it. Plan to attend with your ex. Look forward to it. Be prepared. It is the best opportunity to see your child's school environment, her progress, her areas of concern, and have one-on-one communication with your child's teacher. It is very important that both parents are listening and participating in the same conversation.

Before scheduling the conference, check with your ex to ensure that the time is feasible for him. You want to schedule a time that is best for both of you, where you can be focused and not rushed. Usually, conferences don't last for more than fifteen minutes, so being late is not an option; be sure to allow for traffic.

During your reminder call to your ex, take the time to discuss your child's schooling. Bring your ex up to speed on the latest projects, tests, and classroom friendships. You want him to be aware of any problems or concerns so that the two of you can address sensitive subjects with the teacher. If a classroom problem does exist, then think of possible solutions together so that you are better prepared to develop a solution with the teacher. You and your ex are a team. Your child's teacher can best teach when she knows that there is shared interest in your child.

Once at the conference, sit next to each other so that you can look at reports, journals, tests, and other notes together. If you would like copies of the materials for your separate files, then photocopy them yourself after the conference is over. Listen to the teacher's remarks and respond appropriately. Have respect for your ex's comments, and work as a team with the teacher to resolve any issues. At the end, thank your child's teacher and your ex for a successful conference. Invite her to call on either one of you if additional issues arise.

Don't let your divorce get in the way of your child's schooling. Your child can only benefit when her mom and dad are a cohesive unit, both actively participating in her school affairs.

Divorced Situation 21

PARENTS TOGETHER: Visits to the Doctor

Few things are more stressful than a trip to the doctor's or dentist's office, except maybe an office visit that also includes two divorced parents. During these stressful times in your child's life, how will you behave? Will you allow your divorced emotions to flare up, or will you nurture your child as Parents Together?

The Old Way

As you go to schedule the doctor's appointment for your child, you pause as you contemplate who to dial first: your ex or the doctor. You think about the doctor's office: a room no larger than your bathroom. A size that is certainly far too small to accommodate a doctor, your child, you, and your ex. Being in the same building as your ex is pushing the boundaries; being in the same doctor's office is out of the question. There is no way that you are going to consult with him about this appointment time.

As you're dialing the doctor's office, you're hoping that the first available appointment is convenient for you and impossible for your ex to attend. You can blame it all on the doctor's office while rejoicing in the result. Sure, you'll let him know what happens at the appointment, but as far as you're concerned, you are the one that is responsible for your child's medical care. Your attitude is this: your ex's right to involvement ended the moment you got divorced.

♡

It is unimportant if the doctor knows that the two of you are divorced. It is only important that the doctor knows that you are concerned and interested parents.

The *Pro ♥ Child* **Way**

When your child is ill or facing a surgery, it is critical for both parents to be involved in all medical aspects, including visits to the doctor. By both of you being present and involved, not only are you demonstrating your love to your child, but also you provide another "set of ears" to listen to and ask questions of the medical provider. When scheduling these specialist appointments, be considerate of your ex's schedule. When possible, arrange appointments when both of you are able to attend.

For routine appointments, like well-child visits or dental cleanings, it may be difficult to determine if both parents should be present. When questioning whether your ex should attend, consider how you would have handled the appointment before the divorce. If both parents regularly attended routine physicals, then that should continue. If Dad only attended specialist appointments, then that should continue. But certainly if an emergency or serious illness occurs, both parents should be actively involved, holding their child's hand throughout.

During the office visits, both you and your ex should participate by asking and answering questions. If you know that your ex has unresolved concerns, then prompt him to address it. You are both there as advocates for your child. It is unimportant if the doctor knows that the two of you are divorced. It is only important that the doctor knows that you are concerned and interested parents.

When traumatic medical decisions need to be made, take time to be with your child. Both parents should explain treatment and provide loving arms of comfort. Assure your child that both parents agree on the treatment and are confident in the doctor's decision. Let your child know that you are both there for her and that you will face all procedures together. Your words are promises to her; your actions of being there together for her is her proof.

Divorced Situation **22**

PARENTS TOGETHER: Your Child's Wedding

Instead of eloping, your child and fiancé decide to celebrate and have a wedding! When your child's dreams fill with wedding day bliss, how does she picture her parents? The video camera will be there to capture every moment. Will you and your ex only be caught in a panning view, or will you be there to celebrate this special day focused on your child?

The *Old* Way

Weddings are famous for being chock full of stress. Add a couple of divorced parents and you know the whole affair is doomed for disaster. Instead of a day of which your daughter dreams, it is a day that you know she dreads. Sure, she likes the groom and wedding-dress part, but the rest of it is a wedding planner's nightmare.

The complications begin with the invitation and don't stop until the last dance of the evening. Big questions become big issues. Whose names are listed on the invitation? It certainly isn't going to read, "Mr. & Mrs. Happy Parent are pleased to announce…." And, who is paying for what? You naturally thought that the expense was your ex's responsibility, and it turned out your ex hadn't thought of it at all. The end result for your child is no money, not twice the money. Who is walking the bride down the aisle? How dare your lacking ex now think that he can strut down the aisle when everyone knows how much you have been through. How are seating arrangements being handled? Your table at the reception will be far away from your ex's table, and it's for sure that yours is going to be right up front.

Of course her stepparents just complicate the situation further. Your husband, her stepdad, has practically raised your daughter, so why shouldn't he walk the bride down the aisle? Where does the step-monster fit into the wedding plans? Can she sit in a closet?

A divorced-parent wedding is complicated. You feel for your child, but divorce is what it is. She knows to expect it. All the events that have required both her parents' involvement have ended in flames, and a wedding is likely to be no different.

♡ *This day is truly a blessing and a testament to your nurturing relationship as Parents Together.*

The *Pro ♥ Child* **Way**

Just like the birthday parties, the holidays, the school visits, and the special activities, this day is about your child, not two divorced parents. All little girls deserve to dream about their wedding day. Teenage sleepovers should be filled with girl talk of fantastic wedding plans. An engaged woman should be giddy with excitement over her upcoming "big day." She should be worried about her hair, not whether her divorced parents are going to behave.

Chances are, your child is going to get married someday. You want that to be a wonderful occasion for her. So start laying the foundation now, so that your divorce is a non-issue at her wedding. If you and your ex raise your child in the Pro♥Child Way, your divorce will naturally be a non-issue as her wedding approaches. She will see the respect and consideration between her divorced parents and naturally expect that will continue at her wedding. She has experienced special events before where her parents have acted as parents. She knows that when it comes to her, her mom and dad are not divorced parents, they are just parents. Your child's wedding is a day for you and your ex to be proud and celebrate together.

As a reminder, here is what parents do at their child's wedding. They plan together. They discuss a budget together. They sit together. They include and honor each other's friends, whether it is a boss or a girlfriend. Parents dance together with the bride and groom. They stand next to each other in the receiving line and make appropriate introductions. They take pictures together with the wedding couple. They laugh and are joyous over their child's wedding day.

When stepfamilies are involved, they should be recognized as special people in the wedding family. Throughout your child's life, loving relationships should have been fostered between your child and her stepmom and/or stepdad. These individuals are a critical part of your child's sense of being and an unmistakable part of her life. Of course they should be included. Think of treating them as you would a loved grandparent. They should be seated with the family, included in the receiving line, be adorned with flowers, participate in any family pictures, and be a welcome and natural part of the celebration.

A wedding should be chock full of love. Love between a bride and groom, parents and their child, extended family, and friends. At this happy occasion, there is simply no room for anything but love. This day is truly a blessing and a testament to your nurturing relationship as Parents Together.

SECTION 3

COMMUNICATION:
Communicating with Your Child and Your Ex

A Few Words About Communication

When going through a divorce, it is one thing to "go through the motions" with your child and your ex. After reading a couple Pro♡Child Way entries, perhaps you've decided that you can force your hand to flop up and down in a motion that signifies good-bye, or even make your mouth turn upward – which, to some, means a smile. These physical gestures can be done, even as your teeth are grinding. The goal, of course, is for your child to interpret these as loving, wonderful, positive, "have a great time with your Dad!" gestures. Only you know whether your heart is into these gestures or not. Only you know what is going on in your mind.

It's quite another thing to talk the walk. While your child is paying attention to what you **do,** she's also affected by what you **say**. Sometimes, in divorced-parenting, it is easier to **do** than **say** … but **say** you must. And just so you're clear, saying, "You're father is a real jerk," isn't exactly the Pro♡Child Way.

Think of **doing** as little quizzes; **saying** is the test. You can maintain your high grade if you perform well on your routine **doings,** but you can fail the whole class by bombing on one big **saying**. Watch what you **say**. This is critical when you're talking to you child. And, truth be told, it's important when you talk to your ex too.

In your divorced slump, you may be wondering why you must **say** anything at all, but reality will eventually dictate and you'll have to **say** something. Your child notices silence. Through your silence, your child quickly understands that talking about her dad is a no-no subject. When your child can't talk to you about the things that are going on in her life, it affects her.

So, it's time for you to include communication in your Pro♡Child "to-do" list. By looking at your child and seeing her smile, it's amazing what you can do. You can do this. You can talk nicely about her dad to her. You can tell her that you and her dad love her. You can talk about the divorce as a gentle topic. You can even tell her that you and her dad talk about her … all because you love her very, very much.

Whether talking to your child or talking to your ex, the key word is "communicating." Sharing ideas, inviting input, listening and not judging – these are the essential ingredients to communication. What is the goal of this communicating? To shape, guide, and promote your child's happiness.

> *What is the goal of this communicating? To shape, guide, and promote your child's happiness.*

Divorced Situation 23

TALKING TO YOUR EX: Your Child Should Know That Her Parents Talk

Once the divorce is over, it's very tempting to cease communicating with your ex. You may be ready for an ex-free life, but remember that while your life with your ex is over, your child's relationship with her dad continues. Keep your activities and thoughts about *your* life to yourself, but when it comes to your child, recognize that she has two parents. Resist an environment of secrecy, and talk with your ex about your child. Your child needs to know that her parents talk.

The Old Way

Why should you tell your ex anything about your child? After all, if he was really that interested, he shouldn't have divorced you in the first place. Tough luck that he now doesn't know what is happening in his child's life. That's what he deserves. He wasn't interested in her life before, and you surely aren't going to go out of your way to inform him now. He'll be sorry. Imagine how embarrassed he will be when he runs into her teacher and doesn't even know her name. Boy, then everyone will realize how little he knows about his own child. He's such a joke.

Maybe she'll tell her dad about the big project at school that she turned in yesterday. Won't his mouth drop when he hears that it was on his favorite topic and he totally missed the whole thing! Maybe he'll learn that he should actually *ask* his child what is going on in her life? Would it kill him to pick up the phone and call his daughter? If he wants to be more involved in her life, he's got to do the involving. Until then, he'll remain the totally uninvolved father that he's always been. She's used to it.

♡ *Your child should grow up knowing that her mom and dad share the good, the bad, and the mundane.*

The *Pro ♥ Child* Way

Not only is it important that you and your ex regularly talk about your child, but it is also equally important that your child is aware of it. Your child should regularly hear phrases such as: "I talked to Dad today..." and "I'll have to ask Dad what he thinks about..." and "Dad laughed when he hears..." and "Dad will be so proud when I tell him...."

Your child should grow up knowing that her Mom and Dad share the good, the bad, and the mundane. When the tale-to-tell is a good one, your child will feel great that "Dad knows too." When the tale-to-tell is a mundane one, your child feels secure knowing that even her everyday issues matter to both her parents. When the tale involves a concern or a problem, your child is aware that "Dad will know too."

In a Parenting Together relationship, your child will not be able to play Mom against Dad, because Mom and Dad are a part of "Team Her." Is your child threatening that she's going to "tell Dad" about some perceived deficiency of yours? "That's fine," is your response, adding, "You can always talk to Dad about what happens in your life. When I talk to him about it, I'll mention that you want to talk to him as well." Tattle-tale problem solved.

The discussions that you have with your ex should be done privately, out of your child's earshot. Regarding your child's issues, you should be free to discuss and share opinions with your ex. Be considerate of your ex's time by asking him if he has a moment. Did your child do well on a test? Call Dad and tell him, so that he can congratulate her. Is she having trouble with a girl at school? Call Dad and tell him, so that he can watch for signs of trouble or offer advice. Is she chronically stretching bedtime and it's becoming an issue? Call Dad and tell him, so that he knows that it is happening at your house too.

When you relay your conversation to your child, keep it short. The point is simply for her to know that you talked to Dad. Nothing heavy, just a light comment will suffice. "Talked to Dad today, he was really excited to hear about your good grade." Or, "I mentioned to Dad how the girl at school is bothering you. Did anything happen today?" Or, " When I talked to Dad, he had a good suggestion about bedtime." Communication between Mom and Dad should be an expected, ordinary event for your child. She should not have a secret life at Mom's house and a secret life at Dad's house. You can only be an effective parent if you share the issues that involve your child.

Divorced Situation **24**

TALKING TO YOUR EX: Keep the Conversation Focused

You realize that it is important to share information regarding your child with your ex, but it seems that every time a conversation starts, it gets out of hand. Your ex starts blaming, bashing, and accusing you, which causes your emotions to explode. Sometimes it seems that it would be better if you didn't talk at all. Well, perhaps it would be better for you. But where is your child's benefit in having two parents that can't have a simple conversation about her? When you choose to communicate, do it the Pro♥Child way.

The *Old* Way

All you want to do is tell your ex that your daughter had one cavity discovered at her dentist visit today. It seems like a simple, matter-of-fact statement, but you dread making the call. It seems that every time you talk to your ex, it ends in disaster.

As your heart is racing, you hear him say hello and you start stammering about the weather. You can hear the work noise in the background and you realize that you called at a bad time. Shoot, he's stressed. You quickly state that she has a cavity and then keep talking about how she brushes her teeth regularly and flosses and that you stay on top of it and don't know how the cavity happened and maybe it's the style of toothbrush and you need to buy a different kind of toothpaste … until you pause long enough to take a breath.

He jumps in with his ideas, starting with his favorite topic: blaming you. Before you know it, he's going on about the general lack of structure and routine in your child's life and that it's a wonder all of her teeth aren't falling out. He's stressed about the cost of all the dental care that she'll need in the future and starts questioning whether you're equipped to be an effective mother.

Your head begins to spin and you are hating yourself for even calling. You're getting so angry that once again this has turned into a problem with **you**. You've had enough. This time, it's time to fight back.

The purpose of communicating with your ex is to create a better, nurturing relationship for your child. Do it often and with sensibility.

The *Pro* ♥ *Child* Way

Unless you and your ex have already graduated to free-flowing conversation (which may happen after 20 years), it's best to keep each conversation to a single issue concerning your child. After all, if he were the Great Communicator, you probably wouldn't be divorced. Assume that he can't handle more than one topic, stick to it, and then shut up.

An opportunity to talk doesn't mean an open forum to rehash the particulars that lead up to the divorce, his perceived lacking interest in his child, or his other poor choices. Instead, you want focused conversations regarding your child, not regarding your ex. Keep the conversations manageable, short, and on topic. Here are some appropriate topics: the clothes that she will be taking to Dad's house so that she'll be ready for pictures when you pick her up; her homework that needs to be completed while at his house; or a reminder of an upcoming teacher conference. Notice that none of these topics included the proverbial kitchen sink.

Remember that it takes two to start talking off the subject. If he starts leading down the path of rehashing old issues, don't respond. He can try to have a conversation by himself, but will quickly give up if you're not playing along. Simply state the purpose of your call again, and redirect back to topic. You don't have to be nasty about it, just direct. "So, will you be able to help her study her spelling words or do you want to drop her off early so that I can help her?" After a series of conversations that remain focused and on topic, it will get easier. He will realize that a call from you doesn't mean a free-for-all. You have the magical ability to end any call by hanging up. Eventually, once a feeling of safety has returned to your conversations, you will be able to have more light-hearted, free-flowing conversations.

When "big" issues arise, give your ex some notice. Let him know that you wish to discuss a "big" issue, and ask when it would be best to talk. "Hey, I want to share with you some concerns about our child's behavior at school. Is now a good time?" Perhaps a "heads-up" email is best. While email should not replace a conversation, it can be used as a starter to find a good time for the necessary phone call. Be cautious and safe when composing. Never send a hateful message. Imagine your child reading it someday.

If the issue is too big to handle, consider involving an independent mediator. The procedural guidelines for mediation will help keep the conversation focused and non-threatening. This will allow the two of you to decide on a mutually acceptable solution. By going to mediation, you are not signaling that you are an incapable human being; instead you are demonstrating that you are a concerned parent that will go to any means to make a better environment for your child. Take charge by setting up the appointment and inviting your ex to participate. Reschedule if necessary, but keep scheduling until he attends. Your child is worth your effort to communicate with her dad.

The purpose of communicating with your ex is to create a better, nurturing relationship for your child. Do it often and with sensibility.

Divorced Situation 25

TALKING TO YOUR CHILD: Saying "I Love You"

It's easy to get caught up in the routine of life. Cooking, cleaning, working, transporting. And through it all, your thoughts are still filled with divorce – what went wrong, what you should have said, what he should have done. Take time away from your head and take note about how you feel towards your child. You feel love. Typically, this goes unsaid. Purposefully, love her and tell her about it. Tell your child that she is loved.

The Old Way

When was the last time you told your child, "I love you"? Typically, it's been far too long. As you kiss your child goodnight, what is the last thing she hears? You whispering, "I love you," or your footsteps walking away?

You prepare her food, you make sure she has clean clothes to wear, you help her with her homework, and you take an interest in her friends. You love your child, and your daily actions prove this love over and over again. But do you say it? Do you say, "I love you!"?

"Of course my child knows that I love her," you rationalize. Maybe she does and maybe she doesn't. If she isn't told, how does she really know that what she sees is love?

What about her dad? When left to the Old Way, divorce often leaves a child questioning whether any love is left for anyone. Does she know that her dad loves her? Again you assert, "Of course my child knows that her dad loves her." Besides, that conversation is on his shoulders. It's up to him to tell her.

> ♡
> It isn't up to you to place judgment
> on your ex's love for your child;
> it's your job to tell her that it exists.

The *Pro ♥ Child* Way

But what if your ex isn't telling his child that he loves her? That's a pretty important item to be left to chance. For your child's sake, get over it and take up the responsibility of telling your child that both her parents love her.

Your child needs to hear that she is loved, over and over again. Your child should know, without a doubt, that her mother loves her. Your child should know, without a doubt, that her father loves her. Both of you, unconditionally, without end. How does your child know this? Because it's what she sees, feels, **and** hears. It is your job as her parent to tell her, every day, how much she is loved by both of her parents.

While actions can speak louder than words, by saying these loving words you show your child that your heart is open to her and that no matter what you do, or no matter what she does, she is loved. She is loved fully, openly, and without reserve. By hearing that she is loved, by you and her dad, she is able to connect what she experiences with what she hears and to create an unquestioning reality.

Establish a routine of love. In the evening before bedtime or in the morning's first smiles, your child should routinely hear how much she is loved. "Do you know what?" you say with a smile. "Mommy loves you very much. Do you know what else? Daddy loves you very much too. Mommy and Daddy both love you very, very much." Start this routine as a baby, and years later, your child will still welcome the playful dialogue. Hearing that both you and her dad love her is always appropriate – even if that love is expressed in different ways.

How comforting for your child to hear this pronouncement of love every day. What you are conveying to your child is that, although there was a divorce, you and her dad love her, and that she is in both of your hearts. Whether near or far, involved or not, love can exist through it all. It isn't up to you to place judgment on your ex's love for your child; it's your job to tell her that it exists.

Divorced Situation 26

TALKING TO YOUR CHILD: Positive Comments About Her Other Parent

Face it. The subject of your child's other parent is going to come up between you and your child. When it is your child who is doing the talking, remember she is also listening. She is hearing what you say about her other parent and she is internalizing all of those words. So what form will your words take? Will you talk about her dad through clenched teeth or through a smile? You get to choose what your child hears from you. Choose the Pro♥Child Way.

The Old Way

You rarely mention your ex's name. There is an understanding that your ex was a part of your past and a bad part, at that. If in a moment of weakness, his name is mentioned, it certainly isn't in a positive light. You hiss his name through clenched teeth and follow it by a string of expletives. The comments that you make about your ex are anything but positive. Everyone in the household knows that it is better to avoid the topic altogether, and they do.

Your child knows, through experience, that mentioning her dad's name brings a wrath of sarcasm and old pain to your surface. She knows that in *your* home, her dad's name is not welcome. And you are just fine with that.

♥
It's so important that your child hear you talk nicely about her other parent.

The *Pro ♥ Child* **Way**

Sure your ex might have been a jerk, but there has to be something nice you can say about him. He has nice hair? He has good hearing?? He can walk in a straight line??? If not, make it up. It is so important that your child hear you talk nicely about her other parent. This is her dad, a person that she loves. You shouldn't "dis" the people that your child loves. And you shouldn't badmouth the people that love your child, especially her dad.

Your child should always hear positive comments about her dad, even if it is as simple as "your dad always brushes his teeth with such care." She doesn't need to know that this annoying habit usually lasted about 20 minutes of every day and night, and gave him the excuse to not change her diaper. What bothered you about your ex could be a welcome trait in your child. Wouldn't it be wonderful if your child suddenly developed an interest in brushing her teeth after hearing this?

So, think of nice things to say. Daily, mention your ex in positive ways. Any way of bringing positive thoughts of your child's dad to her is beneficial to her. You don't want your child's dad to be some abstract, foreign person. You want him to be real, tangible, and ever present in her life and thoughts. "You'll have to tell Dad that joke, he'll love it." "Look at that car, it looks just like Dad's car." "Dad's at work right now, I bet he's eating lunch too." "Your giggle is so nice, it's just like Dad's." "Yum, look at that lobster. Dad loves lobster, too." "You chose to make the flowers blue. Blue is Dad's favorite color." Mention, mention, mention. And by the way, just as you're not to insinuate that your ex is actually a deadbeat jerk, you're also not to insinuate a longing or unrequited love for him. Keep your emotions out of it. This isn't about you. This is about making room for Dad in your child's life. This is about including him in **her** home.

Inevitably, your child will ask you if you love Daddy. If your child ever asks, the answer should be an immediate "Yes, of course! He's your dad. I love everyone that cares for you." Your child has never experienced romantic love and would have no clue what that is. It really isn't necessary to explain the difference. Your child isn't interested in the degree of love, just that you love the person that she loves too. You *can* say this.

Keep the positive comments flowing. Through your consistent remarks, your child will learn to be secure in also bringing up her dad's name. You want to encourage your child to share her feelings about her dad without fear of being attacked or judged. In turn, your child will feel that her dad's presence is an integral part of her life. And you should be just fine with that.

Divorced Situation 27

TALKING TO YOUR CHILD: About the Divorce

When it comes to talking to your child about the divorce, which way is better? "**WHAT?!?**" you silently shriek. "Why would I ever talk about the divorce with my child? Isn't that what we're trying so hard **not** to do??" No. Putting your divorce into perspective doesn't mean erasing it from your child's being. The divorced happened, and like all events that happen to your child, it should be honored and discussed.

The Old Way

It is the event that never happened. With an unconvincing grin on your face and teeth clenched, you assert that everything is "fine, just fine." Your child is fine. Her new life is fine. You are all doing just great. She has adjusted perfectly and it's going to stay that way. The transition worked. She's settled into a routine. The balance is even. Life is merrily rolling along and there is no reason to bring up anything having to do with the divorce. When it comes to your child, there is no need to bring up the "D-word." Ever. That was then, this is now. The past is behind you and your child is moving on.

If it wasn't for all those pesky visitations with her dad, your new lives could easily erase the memory as well as the talk. Those visitations are enough of a reminder to your child that the (divorce) happened; it's so totally obvious that there is no reason to ever bring it up. Some things are better left unsaid.

The Pro ♥ Child Way

News flash: The divorce happened. Everyone knows it. It's not a secret. It happened as sure as you brushed your teeth this morning. Getting to the divorce stage may have been messy, even very messy. But at some point, you and your ex agreed that a divorce was the best solution. For your child, be reconciled in your mind about what happened, not sad, regretful, bitter, or proud. Just acknowledge that it happened. It's for sure that your child knows it happened. She needs your support, not your emotional baggage.

When events happen to your kids, you talk about them. So too should you talk about your divorce. It shouldn't be a daily, long, drawn-out retelling, complete with pictures and diagrams. But it also shouldn't be the event that never happened. Keep it simple and share only the information that your child needs to hear. And listen.

A young child probably won't have much memory of time before the divorce. Instead of burning old photos and mementoes of your marriage, put them in a nice keepsake box. You and your child can occasionally look through this. Your child should see pictures of your wedding day. Mention to your child, "Your dad and I were very happy in this picture. We had such a nice wedding day." Be sure to continue the thought by adding, "Your dad and I are still very happy, even though we are not married anymore." Your child will be proud when you tell her, "everything in this box is very special and I saved it all for you. This is yours and someday you can share it with your children too." If your child is ready for more information, you can add, "Husbands and wives sometimes decide that they can't be married anymore, so after a lot of thinking, Dad and I got divorced. But Dad and I will always be your mom and dad. Nothing will ever change that. We both love you very much and we're so happy that you are in our lives." Through hearing your comforting words and seeing the mementos preserved, your child can move forward, knowing her past is secured.

Your older child also needs to see the past preserved. As more family memories exist, it may take a chest to contain all of the pictures and mementos. Add items and pictures that include her: a paperweight that she made for Father's Day, the pictures that she drew of her family, holiday photos. Of course your child may prefer to display these items in her room, but as childhood things make way for budding interests, family items should be carefully preserved.

Talking about the divorce with your older child takes thought. With an older child, it is easy to say too much. Instead of a monologue, ask your child open-ended questions, letting her tell you what she needs to hear. "Dad and I got divorced because we knew that we would be happier than staying married. And we are happier, which is better for all of us. It was a tough decision, but it was the right one. You know that we both love you very much. What are your thoughts?" Remember that you don't have to tell your child all the "secrets" just because she asked. Show respect for your ex by not revealing any information with which he would be uncomfortable. He should be the one to handle any questions regarding his behavior. You can only discuss your own. No matter the circumstances of your divorce, the fact remains that the divorce happened. Instead of relaying the "before divorce" saga, focus on the "after divorce." The beautiful lesson that you can show your child is how you choose to live your life now. Teach your child that although she may not always have control over what happens in her life, she can control how she responds. Yes, the divorce happened. And yes, there may have been difficult times mixed in with the happy ones, but today you are choosing to move forward by creating an environment where you can all grow in security and love.

You don't have to mention the divorce often, but when mentioned, it shouldn't be a sensitive subject. Whatever words you choose to use, make them gentle.

Divorced Situation 28

TALKING TO YOUR CHILD: Don't Let "Dad" Become "Your Father"

You may wish that you never had to refer to your ex ever again, but in the reality that includes your child, you will. In talking with your child, there will be daily moments when it is unavoidable. You have to refer to your ex somehow; which way will it be? Through your words, you can invite inclusion by saying "Dad" or you can create distance through "your father." Always choose to wrap your child in security by including her "Dad."

The Old Way

You're eating dinner with your child, when she casually mentions that she needs to tell her dad something. Your ears perk up. Did she just mention that person? Without missing a beat, you jump on the opportunity and respond, "Your father blah-blah-blah." And continue with, "That father of yours blah-blah-blah." Anytime you are talking to your child about her dad, it is "your father this" and "your father that." Hey, he isn't your relation anymore and it's for sure that you want no mistaking it. He is after all, *her* father.

As far as you're concerned, "your father" is a lot better than what you want to call him. While tempting, "That jerk is picking you up at 3:00" is a bit over the top, even for you. When your child is around, you have to refer to him somehow. What else are you supposed to call that person?

To your child, Dad is still "Dad."

The *Pro ♥ Child* **Way**

When anyone starts out a sentence with "your father," it just can't be good. When you were growing up, you knew it was going to be bad when your mom started out a sentence with "your father." Even though your parents may have been married, the "your father" phrase was still a sign that trouble was going to follow.

That negative connotation still exists. "Your father" is an inherently negative phrase. Mix it into a divorce situation, and it becomes even more hurtful. What happened to just "Dad"? In relaying thoughts and stating routines to your child, "Dad" worked well when you were married. Continue to use it now that you are divorced. Don't let "Dad" become "your father" just because you are now divorced. Your child didn't divorce her dad.

If you want your child to give something to her dad, tell her, "Give this to Dad," not, "Give this to your father." If your child needs to convey something to your ex, say, "Tell Dad that you lost a tooth today," not, "Tell your father that you lost a tooth today." Include your child by including her dad.

It isn't just word choice; these words have emotions behind them. "Your father" not only implies something is wrong, but also reinforces a detachment from you. You're clearly saying, "What he does has no reflection on me, I'm not related to him, you are." OK, so you're divorced. Your child knows this. You don't need to constantly "detach" yourself from your ex. Everyone knows that when you say "Dad," you mean "the father of your child with whom you are now divorced." The divorce happened, you don't need to bring it into the present every time the opportunity arises.

So, just say "Dad." In your world, the title of "husband" has changed to "ex," but to your child, Dad is still "Dad." It's your child's perspective that matters.

SECTION 4

THE MONEY ISSUE:
Don't Let Money Become the Issue, The Issue Is Raising Your Child

A Few Words About Money

Our children are exposed to a lot of "things." Turn on the TV and there are "things." Send your child to school and there are "things." Take a trip to a store and there are more and more "things." With all the "things," it's easy to see how "things" can quickly become the issue. And it isn't just the children that fall into this trap. Don't forget their teacher: you. What are you focused on? If it is money, then admit it. Admit that you are caught up in the divorce/money mindset. If your divorce discussions are solely focused on money, stop to see what you're neglecting. Learn to turn the focus off of money and place it back on your child. Teach your child that she is important, not the money.

If you were very, very rich and poured money onto your child's every desire, you could love your child, right? Could you still be a loving parent if you chose to limit your child's access to immense wealth? Could your child still feel loved, wanted, and secure knowing that you aren't spending every available dollar on her? Of course, love isn't measured by the amount of money that is lavished on a child.

What if you were very, very poor? With your limited means, could you still love your child? Even in the direst of circumstances where you found yourself in a shelter amongst strangers and lived on the generosity of others, could you still love your child? Would the lack of money mean a lack of love? Or could you still surround your child with love? Of course, even when money isn't there, love for your child can still be found.

Sadly there are children who don't feel any love transcending wealth or poverty. Whether from rich or poor backgrounds, it is possible to grow up without love. No amount of money can buy what they need. Love cannot be forced through money. Money cannot hide an absence of love. Your child doesn't "win" through "things"; your child wins through love.

Loving your child has nothing to do with money. This goes for your ex too. Your ex can love his child through wealth. Your ex can love his child through poverty. He can love his child through extravagance or through frugality. It is only important that your child feels love from her dad. Really and truly, that is all that matters. Really. You can go to others to replace needed food. You can't ask others to replace a parent's love. She does need love. If you can admit that your ex loves his child, then your child is blessed. If that love prompts your ex to be a supportive, providing parent, then your child is very lucky.

Is your ex truly a toxic parent that doesn't care about his child? Doesn't care if she has a birthday or had a bad day? Doesn't care if she has food at lunch or means to buy her prescription? No amount of money can disguise that ugliness. Protecting your child's heart should be your focus. Shine the spotlight on your child, not your ex. Focus on her. By focusing on your ex's lack of contribution, her pain can't heal. Punishing your ex takes away your energy when healing your child is your priority.

If your ex is capable of showing his child love, don't let money stand in the way. Don't **you** stand in the way. The issues of money, divorce, and love are very separate issues. Don't let money become the issue. The issue is raising your child in love.

♡
Learn to turn the focus off of money and place it back on your child. Teach your child that she is important, not the money.

Divorced Situation 29

THE MONEY ISSUE: Child Support

Before embarking on a child support discussion with your ex, make one thing perfectly clear to your ex: you know that your child benefits from receiving his love, and you will never stand between him and your child – regardless of child support. With this ground rule in place, the focus of child support can get off of access to the child and get on to meeting the financial needs of your child. Choose to separate the issues. Choose to teach your child that love doesn't fluctuate with dollars.

The *Old* Way

Child support – just mentioning it gets your adrenaline started as dollar figures dance before your eyes. A fight is brewing between you and your ex, and you're going to be ready. The name of the game is the bottom line, and the bottom line is going to be huge for you. It's payback time for all that your ex has put you through, and he is going to pay dearly. You deserve child support; in fact, law mandates it, and you are going to get every penny that you can. You have hired the best lawyer, and you'll see him in court.

He doesn't have any money? Who cares! That is his problem; he's finally going to have to grow up and face his responsibilities. After all, you are! So he may have to get a better job. Or two. Or three. The only thing that is important is that he pays. And that he pays what he's supposed to and when he's supposed to. You'll see to it that he pays or suffers the consequences. What are the consequences? Oh, he'll find out. He'll figure it out as he's driving away alone on his day for visitation. He doesn't pay? He loses his privilege to spend time with his daughter. It's his choice.

♡ *Your child's need for love from her mother and father never fluctuates, even when the bank balance is low.*

The *Pro ♥ Child* **Way**

Whoa, slow down and take a deep breath. Next, stop calling your friends and your relatives for advice on matters of child support. Their well-intentioned advice of "taking him for all it's worth" needs to be ignored. Of course they are looking out for your best interest, but it's your job to look after your child's best interest. Think about it. What is best for your child? Really think about it. Perhaps a large bank account is best for your child, and perhaps not. What is absolute is this: a constant, loving relationship with her mother and father is best for a child. A child that is surrounded by talk, fights, and courtroom battles over money learns only one thing: love has a price tag. It doesn't feel good to realize that.

Your child's relationship with you and her dad should be completely independent of any ties to money. Support should never interfere with a loving relationship. "You can't see your dad this month because he is behind on his support." Ouch, is that ever damaging to your child. Or worse: "You can't see your dad because he is in jail for not paying your support." Whoa! Your child's translation is likely to be: "Your dad is in jail because of you." How is that best for your child?

Don't be so quick to judge your ex. Think of it this way: things must really be tough for your ex if he isn't able to pay support. It is during those times that he probably needs the joy of his child in his life the most. Your child's need for love from her mother and father never fluctuates, even when the bank balance is low.

But, you are wondering, surely money is involved somehow. Sure it is. Money is always involved. It is one of a number of important issues that needs to be resolved when you get divorced. Just like setting the visitation and holiday schedule, determining child support needs to be done in a thoughtful manner that focuses on your child and doesn't involve your ego.

Prior to getting out the statutes, formulas, and tax records to determine the amount of child support that is due to your child, talk to your ex. Talking to your ex about his thoughts on child support shouldn't be a big deal. If he contributed to his child's upbringing while you were married, he is going to continue contributing after you are divorced … just as your financial contributions will continue as well. A good parent is a good parent – divorce doesn't change that. So ask your ex (or have your mediator or lawyer ask) what he thinks is an appropriate child support amount. Meanwhile, look at your own financial situation. To absorb a divorce, you need be in an independent financial position (which may be due to alimony). Evaluate how much more your child will require beyond your own living expenses. This amount, the amount that is beyond your living expenses or your ex's living expenses, is the additional cost of your child. This is the amount that is up for question. "Who" can contribute "how much" to cover this amount? If your ex's response is enough to cover what you can't afford, then it's a deal and the child support amount is set. If there is a gap between what you can afford and what your ex can afford, it's time to reevaluate the finances.

No, it still isn't time to march into court, however a mediator may be helpful. If you feel that your ex can contribute more towards the child support, then ask him. Perhaps he is not aware of the cost of your child's tuition, activities, or other expenses. Assume that your ex is clueless to the real cost and enlighten him. Your ex's contribution offer is based on his assumptions: if he is assuming the expenses are low, his offer will be lower than needed.

If indeed you feel that your spouse can contribute more, however he isn't willing, then you have a choice to make. Either make up the difference of monies yourself or choose the legal system. Only you can decide if the fight's effect on your child is worth the monetary gain that your child may receive. There is no "one size fits all" answer here. Just know that court proceedings involving child support can be very damaging to a child. It's hard to be "Parents Together" if you're embroiled in a bitter legal dispute. You must be extra vigilant in shielding your child from any discussions involving money. Regardless of what is happening in your divorce, you must be supportive of your child's ongoing relationship with her father.

Certainly, an option is to make up the difference in monies yourself, or cut back on your child's expenses. This is an option that should be considered. You are neither spineless nor a quitter if you decide to take this route for your child. Instead, you may be making a stronger decision to protect your child from the system and preserving the relationship between your child and her father. The system may have formulas for determining the amount of child support owed, but these formulas do not factor in your families' emotional health.

If you feel that your ex cannot contribute more towards support, then the question stops there. If your ex is in a bad spot and not making enough money to support himself, let alone his child, going to court isn't going to make money magically appear. It does not do your child any good to have a father struggling to make support payments. Your ex should have enough monies after the support payment to better his own situation. Your child's life can only improve as your ex's life improves. During lean times, keep in contact with your ex, supporting each other's attempts at improvement and security. A "parenting together" approach will teach your child compassion now, while allowing for a brighter future. When the financial situation changes for the better, continue the support discussions to allow for increased contributions.

As with all areas regarding your divorce, it is important to consult a lawyer to learn of your rights and responsibilities. Remember that the role of the lawyer is to inform you what your options are under the law. You make the decision how to proceed. Once any decisions are made regarding your divorce, they should be formalized in writing and added to your divorce agreement.

Throughout the child support discussions, never lose site of the real purpose: to create a better environment for your child. If money becomes the priority, then your child isn't.

**Divorced 30
Situation**

THE MONEY ISSUE: Extracurricular Activities

You and your ex have come to an agreement regarding child support – but what about the extracurricular activities? They have costs, and the costs need to be paid. Before your child signs up for another event, take time to stop and make sure the money is available. Don't assume that your ex is paying. Be aware that a support agreement is already in place, and honor that. Guide your child within the financial structure, don't encourage her to carelessly abuse it.

The Old Way

You and your ex have determined regular child support, but that is for the everyday stuff, right? What about all of the extracurricular activities? Certainly your child will not be denied her activities and interests! Horseback riding lessons are expensive. Cheerleading is expensive. Gymnastics is expensive. Even intramural softball is expensive. Every season for your child brings new activities, new gear, and new bills. Lucky for you, you have an ex. Your child can do whatever she wants because it's not going to cost you a thing. Another pair of riding pants? Charge Dad. A new sequined gymnastics leotard? Charge Dad. The perfect-fitting catcher's mitt? Dad.

Extracurricular activities equal extracurricular monies. And extracurricular monies equal Dad. Time for him to pay up. That's how it goes when you're divorced: too bad for him.

> ♡ *Guide your child within the financial structure, don't encourage her to carelessly abuse it.*

The Pro ♥ Child Way

Here is how the "old way" translates for your child: "Go ahead and buy what you want. The more you buy for your activities, the more you'll be able to screw Dad." Yikes. Pretty obvious how awful that is, isn't it?

If you are down to issues like "extracurricular activities," then you and your ex have already determined the larger issue of child support. And unless you and your ex have written in an "extracurricular activities clause," then the issue is already settled. Don't go running to your ex with new bills in hand. Child support has been agreed upon. The amount that your child is receiving from your ex is decided. If your child needs money for her activities, then it is your responsibility to handle it. You can take it out of child support, you can pay for it yourself, or you can rethink the purchase. Those are the choices for you to make. If you are accepting child support, then you also need to accept the responsibility that goes with it.

Here is how the Pro♡Child Way could translate for your child: "You are important and so are your activities. I will be responsible in enabling you to continue." Through this, your child will learn valuable lessons by witnessing your responsibility with money management. Your child should know that her dad contributes to her living and that you are responsible for managing that money. Meanwhile, your child can have fun and learn about the benefits of hard work by participating in her extracurricular activities.

Of course there are times when the combination of child support and your monies isn't enough to cover your child's extracurricular activities. When this reality exists, it is time for you and your child to rethink the extras. There is nothing wrong with including your child in the decision to put off an activity. Instead of shielding your older child from financial decisions, include her. When presented in a thoughtful way, your child can learn compassion and responsibility when saying no to an activity. Being able to take five dance classes is a testament to her dedication and talent, but at $60 per dance recital costume on top of the monthly tuition, it's also a financial commitment. Your child should be part of the solution in meeting the obligations. If your budget allows her to take only four classes, what is her solution? Possible choices may include contributing babysitting money or choosing not to take the classes. Remember to share this decision with her dad so that he can be aware of the choice and the reasons behind it. He may be able to help her through any disappointments.

As your child's Pro♡Child parent, there may arise a unique occasion that would be incredible for your child to participate – even though you know the monies aren't available. In these extraordinarily special times, there may be cause to call your ex and discuss the activity. Should you both agree that the event warrants extra spending, and if your ex agrees that the extra spending is possible, then you can both tell your child that you've worked together to come up with a solution.

When it comes to your child's extracurricular activities, the **extra** should not be forgotten. Certainly there are times when your child greatly benefits from participation – and your child's smile is always a great reason to continue – but extra is extra. Just as within an intact family, sometimes money determines participation. Teach your child that you and her dad will always be there to support her, either through her activities or next to her on the sidelines.

Divorced Situation 31

THE MONEY ISSUE: Medical Expenses

When it comes to paying for your child's medical expenses, don't assume that your ex will be footing the bill. As with all financial matters that involve your child, assuming will usually lead you down the wrong path. If you are unsure if you or your ex is responsible for paying, you can choose the Old Way of handling the situation, or you can choose the Pro♡Child Way.

The *Old* Way

Your child needed to see a doctor and as you're leaving the office, the billing specialist hands you the bill – the bill that clearly your ex should be paying! Your daughter needed to see a good doctor. It's not your fault that your ex's inadequate insurance didn't cover the visit. He's paying the bill. Immediately you get your girl-friend on the phone, and you start griping. Girlfriends are great defenders, "What do you mean he isn't paying for her doctor's visit? Call your lawyer!"

There is nothing more satisfying than an outsider coming to your cause. It's just the boost you needed to dig in your heals and get the lawyer on the phone. You are fully justified. If your ex doesn't want to pay the doctor the first time around, he can pay for her doctor and for your lawyer the second time around.

♡ *Honor the financial system that was determined and gratefully work within it. Certainly, your child doesn't care who pays for her needed visit.*

The *Pro ♥ Child* Way

When determining a health care provider for your child, your first thought should be of your child. Who will my child be most comfortable seeing? Most likely your decision will be influenced by several factors, which of course will include the doctor's expertise, but may also include gentle ways, a smile, and a comforting waiting room. As with all people that you invite into your child's life, it is important that your child knows that you picked her doctor with *her* in mind. Another influencing factor is the doctor's cost. Depending on your circumstances, this may greatly influence the providers you consider.

Just because you've determined who is responsible for your child's insurance doesn't mean medical expenses are a done deal. Sorry, it's not the same issue. You still need to decide how medical expenses will be paid.

Keep in mind that insurance varies from plan to plan. "In network," "out of network," "HMO," and indemnity plans all require your unique attention. Does your child's dad carry HMO insurance, but you prefer taking her to another doctor? That is your choice, so don't complain when you receive the medical bill. Did you forget to get a referral before taking your child to the eye specialist? Well, after you've paid the bill, you probably won't forget next time. When making health care choices for your child, do so responsibly. Your ex may be required to provide the health insurance, but unless it's stipulated in the divorce agreement, he isn't required to provide for the doctors and insurance that *you* think are best. If you don't like the doctors that are in his plan, then either pay for your own doctor, find a doctor in the plan that is suitable, or put your child under your own health insurance. Honor the financial system that was determined and gratefully work within it. Certainly, your child doesn't care who pays for her needed visit.

Don't create issues with your ex where there aren't any. Recognize that routine medical expenses happen. Just because a new expense pops up doesn't mean that you can pound on your ex's door. Manage your child's support money in anticipation of routine medical expenses.

For extraordinary medical issues, as "Parents Together" your ex will already be involved. Surgeries, serious illness, or accidents are critical moments for your child that require both parents' attention. During these times, medical decisions and expenses should be shared or handled in the best possible way by both parents.

So, to your friend that championed that demanding phone call to your ex: thank her for all of her support and encouragement, and then remind her that what you really need help in is letting go of the entitlement attitude. Have her help you to find a solution to your child's medical needs that nurtures your child, not antagonizes your ex.

Divorced Situation 32

THE MONEY ISSUE: College Fund and Savings

Perhaps you are one of the lucky ones, financially able to provide for your child's college. If during your married years, you and your ex determined that college savings was an important goal, then nothing should change now that you're divorced. Your joint decision to provide for your child's college doesn't hinge on your marital status. But if you're further behind in the financial planning, you may find yourself divorced with no college savings in place. In this circumstance, how do you proceed? How do you make college a possibility for your child?

The Old Way

College? What college? How can you possibly think of college with everything that is going on? And what about your savings? The divorce wiped out the little savings that you were able to accumulate. If any monies are going to be put towards your child's college or savings, it certainly isn't going to come from you. When the time comes your ex had better be prepared to pay. And you don't mean pay for a community college. Your daughter is private school quality and his money had better be there to do it. It's your ex's responsibility and that's all there is to say about that!

♡
This isn't about who is going to pay how much. This is about your child's future and how you two are going to work together to achieve that goal.

The *Pro ♥ Child* **Way**

Ask yourself, "Are you hoping that your child will continue her education after high school?" If so, it's time for you to start saving now.

Notice I said "you." Of course your ex should also be investing money in your child's future, but that is out of your direct control. You do have control over your own money. You are responsible for your child. You are responsible for your child's future. Don't gamble away your child's future by betting on your ex. While preparing to shoulder this responsibility, actively encourage your ex's contribution.

Communicate with your ex when you are able to place money in savings for your child. And do it nicely. Telling him that you are actively saving for your child's future may encourage him to do the same. If your child is older and college is crashing in quick, then a more proactive solution may be necessary.

Remember that college is not an entitlement. College monies are different than child support money for food and essentials. While your child is blessed if she has a family that can afford all colleges, many intact families struggle to send their child to any college. Work within your means to find the best solution, which may include financial aid, scholarships, or state and community colleges. Include your high-schooler in the discussion. Just remember to support her always, not bashing and blaming your ex for the limited choices. Regardless of your ex's monetary contribution, your child may benefit from her dad's opinions on college selection.

When talking to your ex about savings and college monies, be sure to keep the conversation focused on the best course for your child. This isn't about who is going to pay how much. This is about your child's future and how you two are going to work together to achieve that goal. Most likely, you will not split the cost equally; but hopefully you will share the recognition of this important goal.

Divorced Situation 33

THE MONEY ISSUE: Clothes, Shoes, and Food

The child support bank account can deplete quickly. With so many competing items, it can be difficult for the child support budget to support them all. Although it is valuable for your child to participate in various activities and have extra things, the basics never go away: clothes, shoes, food. When the monies are being stretched, which way do you respond? Do you wrap your child in security, or do you expose her to scarcity?

The *Old* Way

Your child is heading off to Dad's house for visitation. She may not notice that her pants are a little short and her top is a little worn, but hopefully your ex will. You carefully planned this outfit to emphasize how scarce her wardrobe has become. At some point, he has to recognize that her wardrobe is ready for an overhaul. You're hoping that your point gets made and that you don't have to pull out a potato sack for next time. Sure, she may have nicer clothes in her closet, but you're trying to make a statement. Maybe this time he'll take her clothes shopping and see how expensive it can be.

And food? Well, it's close enough to dinnertime – let him feed her! Let him experience what it is really like to be responsible for a child. You could use that extra $5; and besides, you don't feel like making dinner anyway. Life with a child isn't always playtime, and it's about time he experience that. So as your child is walking out the door, you innocently suggest: "Yummmm, wouldn't lobster taste good tonight?" As your child greets her dad, you smirk as she exclaims, "Hey, Dad! I'm starving, let's go get seafood!"

Using the means available,
you are responsible for meeting
your child's needs.

The *Pro ♥ Child* Way

Uhhhhh … child support? Remember that? If you expect your ex to take his child clothes shopping, then stop accepting child support. Your ex is already providing for his child. If that arrangement isn't working out, don't let your child be the subtle messenger.

Child support is for your child's needs. Clothing and food are pretty basic needs for which child support provides. Prior to spending her money on any other activity or item, the basics must be covered. Sure your child's definition of a basic and your definition may differ, but you're the parent, act like it: discern what's best. Crab legs may be better than tuna casserole, but most budgets would disagree. Designer clothes may be nice for special occasions, but on most days, jeans and a t-shirt will suffice. Using the means available, you are responsible for meeting your child's needs. If you are limited to using only child support money, then make sure you work within that budget.

If an overall increase in expenses has outpaced child support, then talk to your ex. Not through innuendoes, but through direct communication. As "Parents Together," evaluate your child's expenses and resources so that her basic needs are no longer depleting the budget. Perhaps your ex is unaware that clothing prices grow along with your child. Gone may be the days of toddler rompers to be replaced with much more costly teenage-size clothes.

When it's time to travel to Dad's house, pull out the better clothes, not the worst. If your ex has bought her a special outfit or a t-shirt from vacation, make sure she gets to wear it to Dad's house. Your child knows that her dad lovingly bought her something and will love wearing it. What's the goal? For your child to always feel loved and valued.

Taking care of your child's needs most certainly includes food. Unless you know that dinner is part of the visitation plan, be sure your child eats! Your child should never suffer because of your ulterior motives. Above all else, you are responsible for your child's comfort and happiness. Ensure it.

Divorced Situation 34

THE MONEY ISSUE: Birthday Parties

As your child's birthday approaches, does a scheming smirk don your face? Does your first thought turn to your ex and how much you can get out of him this time? As you walk by the mirror, take your eyes off of your plans and place them back onto your child: the birthday girl. Give your child a big hug and state how lucky you are since she has been born! When it comes to your child's birthday, your only focus should be on celebrating your child's life.

The Old Way

Now this is where you can really sock-it to your ex. He might balk at coughing up more money for her clothes or activities, but this is her birthday. There is no way he can weasel out of paying for an elaborate birthday party. If he did, he would look like a real loser. If he has any sense of what's right, he's going to have to pay for the best birthday party ever. Besides, he has a lot to make up for – this is one way that he can prove how much he really loves his child.

One thing is for sure: you're not going to pay for this party. That you can guarantee. This time, you're not going to bail him out of his responsibility. If he isn't going to fork over the money for the birthday party, then there simply won't be one. He'll look so bad. He'll have to explain to everyone why he is such a jerk. "Imagine that," everyone will say, "your ex won't even pay for his own child's birthday party!" No one will ever side with him again. This time, you have him trapped: he'll pay, one way or the other.

♡ *Whether a homespun celebration or an extravagant gala, the point of a birthday party is to demonstrate to your child how very special and loved she is.*

The *Pro ♥ Child* Way

What are you thinking!? Have you lost all sense of caring for your child? A child should not have parents who "trap" each other in plots. A child should not have parents who measure love by money. A child should not have parents who gamble on her birthday party, reveling in the fact that it might not happen!

Your child's birthday is a hallowed occasion. The day of her birth should be marked by love and celebration – regardless of cost. Whether a homespun celebration or an extravagant gala, the point of a birthday party is to demonstrate to your child how very special and loved she is. The point of the day is not to embarrass or test someone that your child loves.

When it comes to money and your child's birthday party, the simplest answer is this: celebrate within your means. Of course it's nice to have an expensive celebration. It is also nice when your ex is able to share the expenses. But the nicest of birthday celebrations happen when your child is surrounded by friends and family who love her: free of conflict and tension. If an expensive celebration is going to cause conflict between you and your ex, then avoid it. Arguments over money are not worth it, because the ultimate cost will be borne by your child.

First off, plan within your budget. Clearly you can't be in conflict with your ex if you're not spending his money! If you feel that your ex may be willing to contribute to the event, discuss it. Define a clear budget, including how much he is willing to contribute, and then stick to it. Never spend your ex's money without his consent.

Instead of a glossed-over, superficial event, strive to give your child a real birthday present – an event where both her mother and father are there – relaxed, comfortable, and smiling at their daughter. Keep the divorce out of it, and focus on creating a great day for your child.

Divorced Situation 35

THE MONEY ISSUE: Extras – Presents for Others, Tickets for the Circus

Will it never stop!? Your child's expenses go on and on and on – money for this, money for that – it's an endless revolving door. Just when you have the budget finalized, another expense pops up. What is the solution to all of these expenses? Resist the temptation to peer into your ex's bank account. Choose to handle the responsibility.

The Old Way

The "can you come to…" list is mounting for your child. Her one friend wants her to come to a birthday party; her other friend wants her to go to the circus; another wants to stop for ice cream after school. Your child may see it as fun with friends, but you see it as money here, money there. While it may only be $5 here and $20 there, the extras are draining you and you've had enough. Besides, when was the last time you went to the circus or bought a present for a friend? Probably, you can't even remember.

Here's your solution to all this needed cash: "Go ask Dad." After all, these are just small items. Certainly your child can ask her dad for a couple dollars for this or a couple dollars for that. After a few "this and thats," all these extras can be taken care of. You're pleased that you derived the perfect solution. And if your child asks her dad, instead of you asking your ex, success is guaranteed. You figure that he must have the extra cash, so what can it hurt. Your child needs some extra money, and he has extra money. Why should you get involved?

Teach your child that you support her involvement with her friends, her activities, and her interests. The value that she gets from these doesn't change by the amount of money spent.

The *Pro ♥ Child* Way

Keep in mind this key item: It is ultimately your responsibility to provide for your child. You can only control you. You can attempt to control your ex. You can even have the courts attempt to control your ex. But in the end, it comes down to you. Whether you are in control of support money or only the money that you can provide, it is up to you to see that your child's needs are provided for. It is not your child's responsibility to ask her other parent for more money every time an extra need arises. Don't make her do your dirty-work.

"Extras" will always pop up, so if possible, budget for them. You want your child to be involved in activities and sports. You want your child to socialize with friends. But with this involvement comes fees, passes, tickets, gifts, plus any number of extra items that cost money.

If your child is receiving support money, you are responsible for providing for your child's ordinary expenses. Don't look at each birthday invitation or each traveling circus to be an excuse to guilt your ex into increased monies. "Extras" are already included in the child support.

When times are tight, it can be heart-wrenching for a parent to say "no" to these little items, especially when it would be so good for your child to be involved. But, sometimes, "no" is the best solution. Stay convicted when lovingly conveying this to your child. If possible, consider alternative solutions. Instead of going to the birthday party, invite your young child's friend over for a zero-cost play-date. Your older child may not have the $6 banana split money, but would she still want to go and get a $2 lemonade? Maybe the church has a scholarship fund to help with the cost of the $50 retreat. Maybe she takes money to buy admission to the football game but takes her own soda to drink. Maybe instead of entering the horse show, she goes along to volunteer. The lesson is for you to teach your child to benefit from life by participating in it, not just buying into it.

When "no" just isn't the best option, as "Parents Together," you and your ex should work towards a solution. But note that asking your ex to further contribute to expenses is something that is only done during the rare tough times. And further note that you are the one doing the asking and discussing. Don't let your child hear any discussions involving money and her. However, should your ex agree to contribute, be sure to express your gratitude to your child. "I think it is really great that Dad was able to help out so that you can take this skiing trip. Be sure to thank him as well."

Take responsibility for your child's expenses: both the large and the small, the needed and the extras. When monies fall short and you decide the need is worth involving your ex, explain graciously and be prepared for both the "yes" and the "no." Respect the decision and move on; show understanding with a "no" and show gratitude with a "yes." Refocus your attention back onto your child.

Teach your child that you support her involvement with her friends, her activities, and her interests. The value that she gets from these doesn't change by the amount of money spent.

Divorced Situation 36

THE MONEY ISSUE: When Times Change, So Should the Support

As times change, so may the economic dynamics of your child's families. You may enjoy a significant increase in salary. Your ex may celebrate the arrival of twins. With all of life's ups and downs, it's bound to affect the monies available. When major events impact the family situation, your attitude towards child support should change as well. Choose to teach your child lessons in compassion and balance.

The *Old* Way

Your ex is going through a financially tough time, so the child support needs to decrease? Hah! You don't think so. Not in a million years. So what if he is going through a tough time? That is his problem, not yours. He's to pay child support, and nothing is going to stop that. In fact, now that you're paying attention, you're going to be extra observant that the support comes not a day late and not a penny short. He lost his job? Tough. His new wife had another baby? Tough. He had a fire at his house? Tough. It's not your problem. He has to pay child support, and pay is what he is going to do. No way are you going to let him get out of his obligations. Your child came first, and first is how the support money is going to rank.

♡ *When tragedies or hardships befall a family, all members pitch in to see it through. That is what being in a family is all about.*

The Pro ♥ Child Way

It is wonderful if you and your ex have been making an honest effort to provide for your child. When your child knows that both parents are being financially responsible, it demonstrates love and respect for a commitment. For these parents, it is important to acknowledge the financial good times and also to share in the bad.

If one parent, who was contributing to support, suddenly loses a job, it is only right to cut back the amount of child support. The newly unemployed parent will need resources to carry him through till a new job is found. It doesn't do your child any good if her honest father loses his job, followed by his car, followed by his house, while she continues to receive full child support. The priorities need to be weighed. In an intact family, all members would have to cut back on expenses during an income loss. As you watch your ex go through these economic hard times, offer assistance and assure your child that you will all work together to see the times through.

Or, if your child's contributing parent has a change in his family such as the birth of twins, temporary bed-rest, or issues that change the household economics, it is time to temporarily cut back the amount of support. When possible, support should ebb and flow to accommodate changes in family economics. Again, think about the situation through the eyes of an intact family. When a new sibling is born, there is always less money available. Love may grow with each new family member, but often the income does not. Until the income and expenses stabilize, consider reducing the amount of support if possible.

When tragedies or hardships befall a family, all members pitch in to see it through. That is what being in a family is all about. Even though your child's family lives in separate households, the effects should be the same. If times are temporarily tough for a part of the family, then all should downgrade their expectations. You want your child to grow up feeling a sense of belonging, and part of that is also feeling compassion. A child who is completely shielded from money concerns becomes greedy, selfish, and detached from those around her. Raise your child to be sensitive to the needs of others, including her family.

Of course, your child's basic needs do not change, but it is the extras that should be looked at. A trip to the amusement park may still be possible, but maybe the games and extra cotton candy can be left out. It is through these smaller items that a child can feel as if they are helping. Encourage your child to be compassionate without making her feel guilty or worried.

Stay in communication with your ex. If you feel that you can absorb a temporary decrease in the amount of child support, then make that offer. As the money becomes available, readjust until the full support is realized. Likewise, if a supporting parent enjoys a significant increase in money, then that too should affect the child. In this latter case, order your child a double scoop of ice cream at the fair!

SECTION 5

BEYOND THE
THREE OF YOU:
Extended Families

A Few Words About Extended Families

Your child's family may encompass many people. This may include step-parents, step-siblings, half-siblings, step-aunts and step-uncles, step-grandparents – the list is only limited by the size of a growing family. When step-parents are added to the clan, your child's extended family number explodes.

With the addition of each new family member, new relationships are formed. Your child's initial response and subsequent relationship with each new person is greatly influenced by you. So your first step is this: you need to decide how you want your child to know others. Do you want your child to know your ex's relations though her love or through your anger? Getting to know new family members is a challenge for your child; don't complicate the issue by interjecting your issues and bias. Perhaps your relationship with your ex's extended family is a positive one and maybe it isn't: that isn't important. What is important is your child's relationship with her whole family.

Your child is a great kid, right? A kid that loves to play, interact, explore, and receive hugs. Don't cut your child out of possibly expanding these opportunities by imposing your negative attitude on her extended family. When it comes to extended families, what is best for your child? Love. Your child benefits from your love, your ex's love, and all the love that may potentially come from others. Don't look at each person as an intruder, but rather as a welcome addition to your child's life. Even when it means biting your tongue, you must consciously encourage your child's loving relationship with each new family member. Don't we all want our children to grow-up in love?

Your child benefits from your love, your ex's love, and all the love that may potentially come from others.

BEYOND THE THREE OF YOU: Your Ex's Spouse

Realize this one thing: you have absolutely no choice when your ex becomes involved with a significant other. Your ex is never going to ask your permission for a potential step-parent to enter the picture. That decision of "who" and "when" is your ex's alone. You can't pick her size, shape, or attitude. This isn't a restaurant: You can't order your child's step-parent. You get what you get – and so does your child. So, when this person is added to your child's life, what will your reaction be? You have a choice: will you help your child in the destructive old way or in a positive way?

The *Old* Way

What do you think about when you hear the words, "your child's step-mom"? Anger. Resentment. Bitterness. As far as you're concerned, this person is just one more reason to dislike your ex and begrudge your child having to spend time at her dad's house. Any woman that your ex brings into your child's life needs to be regarded as suspicious and manipulative. She may think that she has everyone fooled, but not you. You have her type figured out, and there is no way that she is going to worm her way into your child's life. She may have won over your ex's heart, but she isn't going to win over your child – you won't allow that to happen! You are the mom, not her. She is going to know that she isn't welcome or wanted in your child's life. Your only goal is to make her life miserable and for your child to be the messenger.

> ♡ *Your child needs love from all of her family members, and that includes her step-parent.*

The *Pro* ♥ *Child* Way

What should your child hear when she hears the word "step-mom"? Well, for starters: fun, adventures, security, love, and chocolate-chip cookies. Smiles should erupt every time her step-mom is mentioned. Your child should enjoy spending time with her step-mom. Why wouldn't she?

In answer, a probable reason that your child dislikes her step-mom is **you.** Your attitude greatly influences your child's attitude. If you are displaying anger, resentment, and bitterness, then your child will do the same. Your child will naturally want to please you by parroting what you say. Why would your child enjoy baking cookies with someone that you say is awful? Instead of actively participating in measuring out the sugar, your child may sass-off about the "dumb" cookies and "dumb" her. Your reflected attitude may cause your child to miss out on many great experiences. Keep your negative comments in check. Don't spoil your child's relationship with her step-mom.

This is not about you. In every divorced-parenting situation: it is not about you and it is not about the divorce; it is only about your child having great relationships with those that love her. When it comes to your child, you need to switch off your negativity and tune into your child's needs. Your child needs love. Your child needs love from all of her family members, and that includes her step-parent.

But, I hear you ask, what if the step-parent really is rotten? Face it, not all people are nice. Whether the offending person is a step-mom, a teacher, a soccer coach, or a future boss, your job is to teach your child to see the best in everyone by guiding her through steps of understanding. So the soccer coach screams more than you like, or requires exercises that you wouldn't prescribe, or doesn't offer that important positive comment – how would you help your child cope with the coach's behavior enabling her to still gain from the practices? Listen to your child's complaints and then offer other ways for her to see the situation. Agree that running 10 laps around the field is hard, but just think of how easy a game will feel after all the training! Agree that the coach does talk gruff, and offer that maybe that is just how he talks – not actually meaning to be mean or hurtful. In the case of a step-mom, maybe she is offending, but with your guidance your child can still gain and learn from that relationship. In life, you usually can't pick your boss, your teacher, your coach, your mother-in-law, or your step-mom – but you can choose how you deal with each situation. Teach your child to gain positive experiences out of not-so-positive people.

But to hear the stories, it seems that *all* step-moms are bad. Certainly this has to be an exaggeration. Is your child's step-mom really that bad, or through your eyes would any step-mom be unacceptable? Be sure to check your attitude and consciously create the best experiences. Be open and welcoming to others who wish to love and share with your child.

You should take pride when you teach your child to be kind, compassionate, and loving. In return, your child benefits in so many ways. When your child relays that she baked cookies with her step-mom, your response should be an automatic, "Yum! Sounds like fun!" Focus on your child, and encourage your child to delight in the joys of life.

Your child is blessed to have a step-parent that can care, love, and watch over her. Recognize that you greatly influence your child's attitude with her step-parent, and make it a wonderful one.

Divorced Situation 38

BEYOND THE THREE OF YOU: Your New Spouse

Here is the good news, as well as a word of warning: you choose your new spouse. If you walk up the aisle towards marital bliss, the partner on your arm is there because you said, "I do." So, who is this person, and what will he bring to your child's life? Unlike your ex's spouse, you do have control in choosing this person. Don't lose sight that a potential mate can only be a great spouse if he was first a loving potential step-parent to your child.

The Old Way

The violins are playing, fireworks are filling the sky, and your heart is melting. Finally, after such a long and painful journey through divorce, the skies are starting to clear, and the real mate of your dreams is within your reach. You laugh together, you cry together, you share your soul and dreams. You think that this time it will be different. This time you know what you are doing. This time it will be perfect. Only one little hurdle … he doesn't exactly "click" with your child.

OK, you think, this will improve with time. Eventually, she'll warm up to him and he'll be more comfortable around her. Just give it time and all will be OK. If he would just try a little harder, she would see what a great step-dad he will be. If she would just give him a break, he would see what a wonderful step-daughter she will be.

So you plan "family" picnics and dinners, game and movie nights. You smile throughout the evening, but still, the tension is there. At the end of the evening, you're relieved when it is bedtime and your child finally heads up the stairs.

You look on the bright side and say, "Well, we made progress tonight. Next time it'll be better." Your comment is met with a withering look from your potential mate, and you make a mental note to buy a book on step-dad/child relationships. You're not worried though; things will get better between your child and her step-dad. After all, this is normal.

♡ *Make sure that you are choosing a step-parent that not only makes you smile, but also makes your child smile.*

The Pro ♥ Child Way

A tree is being climbed, somersaults are met with applause, and a newly discovered worm is being displayed. Your child is having a great time learning, discovering, and showing off with her friend. Her friend is great to have around. He pays attention to her, shows her new things, and isn't grossed out by her insect discovery. He also is good to have around when the kite gets stuck in the tree or the bicycle gets going too fast. Through all of these activities, she knows one thing: he cares about her.

Oh right, he also cares about you. And you care about him. But to your child, the most important relationship is the one that involves her. Like you, she needs to know that she is important, fun, acceptable, and lovable. She needs to laugh. This man is all the wonderful things that you are looking for in a future mate, including the most important: someone who will make you and your child smile.

Your child's opinion of your choice in mate may not come first, but it shouldn't come second. Your child should have an equally great feeling about her future step-dad. She should look forward to his visits; she should seek out their new adventures; and she should gain security from his love towards you and her.

You cannot demand positive feelings between your child and your mate. It is really up to the two of them to decide if they like each other. It either works or it doesn't. Now of course you can sabotage a good thing, but if you have to orchestrate the perfect situation just to get them comfortable, chances are you'll always be working to keep their relationship cordial. Cordial isn't what Norman Rockwell had in mind when he was drawing a family around the dinner table.

At the end of your guest's visit, if you are feeling relieved that your child is heading to bed, it is a pretty good sign that something isn't right. You've just been through a divorce that was filled with tension; don't start a new relationship where tension is already part of the equation. As you know, all bumps in a relationship can grow into insurmountable barriers. Your child shouldn't be a bump.

The thinking that "they'll grow to like each other" is a thought that went out with "Fiddler on the Roof." You don't want your child to be part of a relationship where she finds herself asking "But, do you love me?" many years from now. Maybe, the question will end in a "yes," but what about all those years lost? Your child's happiness is something that you should strive for daily, not as an end result.

When it comes to your child's step-parent, you do have a choice. You choose by welcoming the mate that has all the right traits. On your long list of attributes, one line is reserved for measuring "step-parent potential." You can check all the other boxes, but when it comes to deciding on this one, leave it blank. You may think that he will make a great step-parent, but only your child can check-off the "great step-parent" box.

You should be committed to making the best choices for your child and creating the best situations where she can grow up feeling loved and secure. Don't lose sight of that goal just because a new person is showing interest in you. You are a package – a very precious package. Make sure that you are choosing a step-parent that not only makes you smile, but also makes your child smile.

Divorced Situation **39**

BEYOND THE THREE OF YOU: Your Spouse's Kids – The Step-Siblings

Drizella and Anastasia: Cinderella's two infamous step-sisters whose names are synonymous with selfish, cruel, and ugly. Is this your image of step-siblings? Or when you think of steps, do you think of Greg, Peter, Bobby, Marcia, Jan, and Cindy – one great big, goofy, good time? It's time for you to choose your child's relationship with your spouse's children, her step-siblings. Get out of the old rut. Choose the Pro♡Child Way.

The *Old* Way

You've gotten remarried, and in addition to a spouse, you now have step-children. Your child now has step-siblings. When you think of your child's step-siblings, what comes to mind? Your image makes Drizella and Anastasia look like angels. As the fairytale suggested, step-siblings are awful, and your spouse's kids are no different. What **is** different is that this time, you're there to protect your child. These step-sisters won't be taking advantage of your precious Cinderella. You are there to shield your child from their demands and from their unruly behavior.

It's for sure you didn't raise these step-children; if you had, they wouldn't be acting like the brats that they are. You hold your tongue to avoid spewing out how lacking their upbringing and manners are – and of course it's their **other** parent that is to blame, not your new spouse. Their other parent is pathetic, allowing her children to behave the way they do. Out in a crowd, you distance yourself and your child away from them for fear that someone might associate them with you. Your child will learn quickly that she isn't to copy their behavior or be anything like them. They are the example of how not to be, and you're there to keep pointing it out.

♡
You're there to cheer on a good relationship between your child and your step-child.

The *Pro♡Child* Way

This isn't about you or your image or even your skills as a parent. This is about being a step-parent. A step-parent who has a child that has a step-sibling. This is about creating the best environment for your child. Your child benefits from each person added – including Drizella.

Step-siblings aren't created, they just exist. Whether they came with your new spouse or your ex's new spouse – voilà, there they are. You may think they are wonderful, adorable, polite, and a joy to be around. Or, you may not. It doesn't matter how they are. It doesn't matter if you think they are Drizella or Marcia. It matters how your child's life is impacted. Your child's life should be enhanced by each new person in it – including step-siblings.

First, a definition to clarify your role as a step-parent. Step-parent: a person who marries someone with children. In other words, you "ain't" the mom and you "ain't" the dad. This child has parents, and it ain't you. Your responsibility to a step-child is primarily one of "cheerleader." You're there to cheer on a good relationship between your spouse and his child. You're there to cheer on a good relationship between your child and the step-child. You're there to cheer on a good relationship between you and your step-child. Unless it is clearly understood that you are to "parent" the step-child, don't. The child has parents, and again, it "ain't" you.

Using this guideline, it is much easier for you to encourage positive relationships between the children. This change in your focus, from "parent" to "cheerleader," is critical. Without it, you could become absorbed in negativity – benefiting no one.

Now, this isn't a "not my child, not my problem" attitude. It is a "come join the fun, anyway!" attitude. Whatever offending trait you feel your step-child possesses, don't let it interfere with your child's enjoyment of them. Clearly Cinderella's step-mother thought Cinderella was a conniving, spoiled brat who was going to keep her own children from excelling. Just imagine how different Cinderella's life would have been if her step-mother would have encouraged Cinderella to play with her daughters instead of serving them. Your attitude greatly affects the tone of the relationship between your child and your step-child. Be sure that your child knows that you expect the whole family to welcome, love, and play with each other.

But what if your step-child is a disaster? When your step-child's negative ways start encroaching on your child's life, you can exert control over your own household. While you should avoid "parenting" your step-child, you can certainly have house rules by which *all* must abide. These house rules might include no eating in the living room, no smoking inside or anywhere your child may observe, no foul language within earshot of your child, or any rule to which the whole family must follow. Be sure your step-child knows that he or she is welcome, but the traits stay outside the door. If your child questions you about a step-sibling's perceived misgiving, go ahead and address it. "What is important is that you know what I expect of you. I expect you to brush your teeth twice a day. I know that your step-sister doesn't, but luckily that doesn't keep her from being a good Monopoly player. I can still love her in spite of that, and you can still have fun together!"

You may roll your eyes at a "teeth brushing" offense – maybe your step-child's misgiving is much more severe. But, so what if it is? The "come join the fun, anyway!" rule covers a whole list of nasty traits. Of course you should never expose your child to imminent harm. The relationship should benefit your child, not endanger her.

Think like Mrs. Brady, and use your creativity and positive thoughts to create environments where your child can have fun and get to know her step-sibling. In turn, your whole family will benefit – especially your child.

BEYOND THE THREE OF YOU: Half-Siblings (On Your Ex's Side)

Your child brings home an assignment from school. On a poster board she is to gather pictures of her family. Anxious to help, you delve into the photo box pulling out picture after picture for her to use. Pleased with your bounty, you place all the photos in front of her. What is her reaction: a smile or a frown? Her reaction largely depends on who is pictured in those photographs: is it *your* family or *her* family? Did you help in an Old Way or a Pro♥Child Way?

The *Old* Way

Household photographs have a funny way of changing quickly after a divorce. The wedding picture gets put away … very far away. The family portrait only slightly misses the trash and is tossed somewhere into the basement. The walls and shelves that once held family memories are emptied.

But not for long; next thing you know, those empty wall spaces are filled with pictures of your new memories – memories that don't include your ex … or his new wife … or their offspring. Wouldn't that be a riot? A picture of your ex and his lovely new family displayed in your home? It's enough to make you gag, isn't it? No, your home is not a showcase for your ex's happy new family.

Your ex may have new children in his life, but as far as you're concerned, your child is the only child that exists. Their children aren't your concern. Your only priority is your child. At his house, the other children may exist, but at your house, your child reigns supreme. It is her portrait that hangs above the mantel … and on the refrigerator … and in her room. She came first, and there is no room for those other children: in pictures or in her life.

You feel sorry that she has to deal with them at your ex's house, and you certainly aren't going to make her deal with them at your house. While your ex may now have to split his love between his new children and your daughter, you're never going to do that. Your child will always know that your love isn't being split with anyone but her. As far as you're concerned, those other children don't exist.

♥ *Reassure your child that a parent's love expands with each new child.*

The *Pro ♥ Child* Way

Realize this, your child's circle of family members is different than yours. Once you get divorced, the image of "your family" drastically changes. Gone are the days of "our family." Instead there is "her family" and "your family." "Your family" includes you and her. "Her family" includes you, her dad … and her step-mom … and her siblings: half and step. All of those people are her family. And if she's lucky, she has a whole pack of extended relatives on all sides of her family. So when the topic of "family portrait" comes up, the first question is: whose? Your child's family is now different than your family.

And this is OK. What hasn't changed is the importance of "family" in your child's life. Belonging to a family is so valuable. It's within families that your child first learns about relationships: for her to feel a part of, included, cared for, and accepted by family members, and for her to do the caring and accepting of her family members. The give-and-take that a family requires is what love is all about. This love lesson is irreplaceable for your child. And just as before the divorce your child participated in this family dance, so should it continue after the divorce. Her family, in all its new forms, still exists: including her half-siblings.

You can't shut out her half-siblings without also denying who she is. Her younger brothers and sisters are part of who she is now. She should be included in the excitement of the upcoming birth and be a critical part of their arrival. If your ex is too busy being a new parent to properly include her, then you need to take up the slack. Buy a "Big Sister" shirt for your child; help your child select a gift for her new sibling; help your child make a card welcoming the new sibling into the world. Do your part by making your child a part. And reassure your child that a parent's love expands with each new child. Her dad has plenty of love to share with all of his children – including her.

As her half-siblings grow, include them in your child's life. It's important that your child knows that these children are just as welcome in your home as they are in their own home. After all, they are her family. And her family should be welcome in her house. In nightly prayers, all of her family should be remembered, including her dad, her step-mom, and her siblings. At your child's important events, all of her family should be included. And on holiday greetings, your child should be proud to be pictured on more than one family's picture card.

Notice that nowhere in this "picture" is your attitude, your judgment, or your opinion. The only "your" that is required is your involvement in creating an inclusive relationship between your child and her step-siblings. Sibling relations can be hard enough on a child. Don't add to the challenge for your child. Support her by supporting her relationships, and perhaps someday you'll be surprised to find yourself tacking up a picture of her and her family on the kitchen refrigerator.

Divorced Situation 41

BEYOND THE THREE OF YOU: Ex-Relatives

Just when you feel that you have a handle on all of the players – your ex, your child, your ex's spouse, your step-children, your child's half-siblings – along re-emerges an ex-relative, and another, and another, and another yet again. Honestly, where do all these relatives keep coming from? As each one grows on your child's overgrowing family tree, do you take out the hedge trimmers or do you go out and buy some training wire? Once again, it's time for you to make a choice: the Old Way or the Pro♥Child Way?

The Old Way

Quick, what's worse than a mother-in-law? You've guessed it: an ex mother-in-law. Aaaagh! What's worse than an ex mother-in-law? An ex mother-in-law who comes with an ex father-in-law plus two ex brothers-in-law with spouses! Aaaaaaaaagh!! Before the ex-ing happened, remember how they used to nag, complain, and point out every single offense that you committed against their darling, perfect baby? Well now that their "darling, perfect baby" is no longer your spouse but your ex, the gloves are off and any restraint that they once showed is gone. Welcome to open-season on you. The worst part is that usually, the weapon of choice comes in the form of threatening child custody action. Nothing bristles the hair on your neck more than an entire ex-family swarming with hysteria spiraling right into your child's life.

You've seen the war brewing and have already hunkered down into your battle station. You've armed yourself with stories of your ex's failings, journals of your ex's misdoings, and even some video that will prove in court that your ex is an unfit parent. One whiff of your bounty should send the whole ex-family into a deep retreat. Now, you're in control. No one is going to top you at the game of slash-and-burn. Your ex is going down, and the destruction of the whole ex-family will only make it more fun. Nothing is going to come in between you and your child – least of all your ex mother-in-law.

♥ *Do what it takes to keep your child surrounded in love. Even if it takes swallowing your pride.*

The *Pro* ♥ *Child* **Way**

True, when you divorce a spouse, you get more than an ex spouse: you get an ex everyone-in-law. But to your child, her grandma is still her grandma. Her grandpa is still the funny joke teller. Her uncle is still a great ballplayer. And, her aunt still painted that really cool mural on her wall. From your child's perspective, nothing's changed. Her family is her family – divorce or no divorce.

If you're having a problem with your ex's family, get over it. If they are having a problem with you, ignore it. Yes, ignore it. It's actually easier than you think to ignore it. It usually requires you to consistently do nothing. Not answering the phone when they call. Not responding to their nasty emails. And not responding to your ex when he brings them into the midst. It is not your job to sway your ex-family to see your point of view. It is hard enough for you to work with your ex to parent the Pro♥Child Way; save your energy and ignore the ex-family. In time, if you stay committed to parenting the Pro♥Child Way, your ex family will calm down. Even the most spiteful ex mother-in-law will have a hard time plotting when her fridge is decorated with your child's sent drawings.

Keep plugging away by telling your child that she is loved by all her family. Reassure your child that her family is always welcome. Repeat her grandfather's bad jokes and remind your child about how much fun it was when she got to throw the ball with her uncle. Build a loving family image. If your ex isn't already doing it, have your child send birthday cards signed with hugs and kisses. Do what it takes to keep your child surrounded in love. Even if it takes swallowing your pride.

Perhaps the feelings between you and them will never be comfortable, but you should always be content knowing you haven't kept your child from running into the arms of a loving grandma.

Divorced Situation 42

BEYOND THE THREE OF YOU: "So Many People That Love You"

As the saying goes, "Actions speak louder than words." True, your actions are a dead giveaway to your true feelings. When your child mentions your ex or her "steps," what is your immediate reaction? If your first reaction is to roll your eyes, then you are sending a hurtful message to your child. You are shutting down all possibility of useful conversation – and replacing any positive thoughts that she may have with your obvious displeasure. Instead, your immediate reaction should be an inviting look that encourages your child to share her thoughts and feelings. From there, the stage is set and your words can have an impact. So what will you say when your child mentions your ex or her "steps"? You can choose to insult and attack them, or you can choose to focus on the love that they offer your child. If you asked your child, which way would she choose?

The Old Way

Some days, you feel so sad for your child. She once had a mom and dad who loved her, and now divorce has split her family apart. Her household is forever ruined. Her dad, who used to be down the hall, is now in a separate house. And his love went with him. You can just imagine how deprived she must now feel.

And now there's **her** – that other woman who is involved in your ex's life. Now his attention is on **her**. What's worse is that she has her own children too! As if it wasn't hard enough for your child to get some love, now more kids have arrived to take time and attention away from her. It's always one more thing. It's all getting out of hand.

You must protect your child from getting hurt. You know what it's like to be wanting love and it not being returned. You're not going to let your child be that vulnerable. Your ex wants a new life? **Fine!** He'll get that new life, and his old life will let him move on. You'll show your daughter that you both are fine without him. He can go and do whatever he likes with whomever he wants – it doesn't affect you or your daughter. The two of you can survive and thrive without them.

Sure, you'll teach her to be polite to them, but it's for sure she'll know that when it comes to love, you're the one that she can count on.

♡ *Encourage everyone to express their love and interests with your child. It is your child that will benefit.*

The *Pro ♥ Child* **Way**

"Do you know what? You are so lucky to have so many people that love you. I love you, Dad loves you, [her dad's girlfriend] loves you, [your husband] loves you, Nana loves you, your brothers and sisters love you, your cousins love you. You are very lucky."

Your child is the luckiest person in the world. She has a mother that loves her very, very much. She has a father that loves her very, very much. With any luck, you and your ex have both found new loves that bring joy and happiness to your child's life. With new people comes expanding love for your child. Your child is indeed very lucky to have so many people that love her.

What more could you want for your child than an additional set of loving arms to hold her, tickle her, or show her the way? A child of divorce shouldn't grow up feeling deprived or less loved. The only reason that would happen is if the adult attitudes mess everything up. Children naturally want to express love and be loved. A step-mom, a step-dad, step-grandparents, or step-siblings are all additional opportunities for your child to be loved. Think of all of the wonderful experiences that these individuals bring to your child's world. Be thankful for their diverse interests and encourage them to share with your child. Encourage everyone to express their love and interests with your child. It is your child that will benefit.

Remind your child often how lucky she is that there are so many people that love her. Your child will grow up feeling safe, protected, and watched over. And most importantly, your child will grow up feeling loved.

Encourage everyone to express their love and interests with your child. It is your child that will benefit.

SECTION 6

BEHAVIOR ISSUES:
Dealing with Discipline
and Behavior

A Few Words About Behavior Issues

When it comes to navigating life at "Mom's house" versus "Dad's house," give your child some credit. Even young children understand that there is "Mom's way" and there is "Dad's way." Parents parent differently. Whether the situation is the bedtime routine, homework habits, or dinnertime customs, parents have different expectations of their child's behavior. Divorced parents are no different. Divorced parents parent differently. You may have tried to reign in the parenting differences while married, but just as that was futile before, it's futile now that you're divorced. Deal with it. It's OK that the different households have different routines. A child adapts. Certainly you can commiserate with your child, sympathizing with her feelings that she doesn't like the way you do things or the way her dad does things, but having compassion for her is different than changing what is.

The same goes for discipline. Moms and dads have different styles. You can't control how discipline is handled at your ex's house, you can only control how you handle your child's acting-up.

Focus on your own household rules instead of nit-picking and micromanaging your ex's household. In divorce, there are some things you can control, and many more that you cannot. Recognize that your ex is responsible for controlling his household, not you. Recognize that you are responsible for controlling your household. Keep any negative opinions as to his household to yourself, not shared with your child. Instead, focus your energy on creating a stable home for you and your child. Focus on teaching your child to handle life.

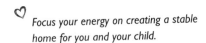

Focus your energy on creating a stable home for you and your child.

Divorced Situation 43

DISCIPLINE: Punishment Shouldn't Cross Households

The road to adulthood is not a smooth one. Whether your child is one or fifteen years old, discipline issues arise almost daily. They happen whether you are divorced or not. Luckily, the majority of issues are of the minor variety. In these circumstances, the rule is simple: if it happens in your house, deal with it in your house. The most effective punishment is an immediate consequence. The most ineffective punishment is a delayed one. Having your child be punished at both households doesn't teach discipline, it only shows disregard for your ex and his relationship with your child. Which way will you parent?

The Old Way

The battle of the day is your young child not wanting to hold your hand when crossing the street. It seems that every day, a new rebellion arises. And every day, it seems that you have less patience to deal with it. So here you are, an arm full of groceries, a busy parking lot, and a three-year-old that screamed halfway through the store. The end is in sight, with the last hurdle only to make it to the car. As you reach down for your child's hand, the response you hear is, "NO!" And with that, the battle has begun. After numerous unsuccessful attempts, your blood pressure is boiling and out it spews, "That's it! No television today and that includes Dad's house too!"

You don't have a three-year-old? Then how about the nine-year-old that refuses to make her bed. You threaten that no friends can come over until it's made – and no friends at Dad's either. Or, the thirteen-year-old that sassed you – you threatened no phone calls or computer for the whole weekend at Dad's house.

You're not new to this. You know that just taking away a privilege isn't enough. Throwing Dad into the equation helps to bolster your stance, right? Besides, he is getting off too easy. He never seems to get the problems; he only gets the fun. He should bear the consequences of real life with his child, too.

♡ *Threatening and demanding that punishment should cross households simply isn't an effective way to teach your child.*

The *Pro♥Child* **Way**

The only good argument for enforcing punishments at your ex's house would be if it was effective. But it isn't. It never was and it never will be. The only thing that this does is create added friction between you and your ex. If your point is to piss off your ex and demonstrate how inept you are, then continue on this path. If your point is to teach your child a better way of behaving, then you need to find another approach. Threatening and demanding that punishment should cross households simply isn't an effective way to teach your child.

So what is a frazzled parent to do? The most effective way to deal with these daily bumps is to deal with them yourself and do so immediately. Your child not holding your hand has nothing to do with Dad. Your child not making her bed has nothing to do with Dad. Your child sassing you has nothing to do with Dad. So why should the punishment involve her time with Dad? Your child is rebelling against *you*. If anything, try to look at it as a compliment. She wouldn't feel the need to rebel if she didn't already think you were an authority. These daily behavior blips are nothing more than her trying to assert her independence from you. It's up to you to decide if the independence is warranted. Maybe when your child reaches age 9, she can stop holding your hand when crossing a parking lot. Maybe your nineteen-year-old can decide if she wants to make her bed. Maybe it will never be OK for your child to be disrespectful to you.

Whatever your decision, make it and make it quick. "No," you may respond back to your three-year-old. "The rule is that you hold my hand when we cross the street. We'll stand here until you are ready to hold my hand." The punishment is interrupting your child's behavior and making her wait. Even if it takes five minutes, you're not budging until she holds your hand. Groceries wilting in the heat should not be a factor. This life lesson is more valuable than a box of melted ice cream. You have one guarantee: your child will not spend her next birthday waiting on that sidewalk. At some point, she will take your hand, probably in a gruff, and you can both walk to the car. As you put your soggy groceries in the car and sit your weary self down, smile. You just taught your child a very important lesson: you mean what you say. If there is a next time, it'll go much smoother. Now she knows that in the end, she'll have to hold your hand or wait an eternity on the sidewalk. Notice that Dad was not involved in the punishment.

How about your nine-year-old's aversion to making her bed? You give your child credit if you think that withholding a play-date many hours from now at Dad's house is going to have any positive effect. Why are you focusing on several hours later? What about the subsequent five minutes? What about now? "No," you exclaim. "You know the rules; nothing else happens until you make your bed." For your information, "nothing else" includes getting dressed, watching TV, reading, drawing, or eating; you get the point – and so will your child. Again, Dad is not part of the discipline solution. Your child will soon learn, or spend a very long time not doing what she'd rather be doing, that making her bed is a non-negotiable part of the routine.

Your thirteen-year-old is the easiest. Teenagers **hate** to be interrupted. Just walking in front of the TV for a mere second of interruption will send one to scream. Again, interrupting her behavior and making her wait until it gets corrected is the most effective punishment that there is. Dad has nothing to do with it. This is your problem to handle. Handle it.

So, let's talk about Dad for a second. The time that he gets to spend with his child is for him and your child to decide, not you. You do not control their time. He does not control your time. If your child and her dad are planning to watch the big game on TV tonight, who are you to say, "No." You have no right to interfere. Punishments should not cross households. If it happens in your house, then deal with it in your house. Don't expect your ex to bail you out.

OK, but what if your child's negative behavior is more than a simple hand hold or bed making? When major discipline issues arise, the basic rule applies: don't insist that your punishment be enforced at the other parent's house. But that doesn't mean you shouldn't tell your ex of the incident or jointly decide on a punishment. Perhaps the behavior was so atrocious that long-term consequences are also warranted. If you and your ex agree that a behavior warrants household-crossing punishment, then together both parents should agree and enforce it. Only after you have discussed it with your ex, tell your child these consequences.

As always, the right answer is the answer that best benefits your child. As always, the wrong answer is the answer that has ulterior motives – such as sticking it to your ex. Appropriate punishment is an issue that all parents continually face. If you need assistance: ask your ex; but don't expect him to blindly enforce your punishments.

Divorced Situation 44

DISCIPLINE: Don't Use Your Ex as a Threat

When it comes to discipline, a good rule of thumb is to leave your ex's name out of any threats or comments that you make to your child — especially a child of divorce. Using your ex as a threat will always backfire, leaving you with a mess to clean up. Your child's behavior will still need to be addressed and you will have a lot of back peddling to do. So, avoid it altogether. Will you fall victim to these phrases or choose the Pro♥Child Way?

The *Old* Way

As you watch in dismay, your child is about to _____. Fill in the blank with your child's latest acting-up moment. The list is as expansive as there are moments in childhood, and it seems that your child is trying to rack them all up in one day. Fed up with it all, you take in a deep breath and blurt out to your child:

(#1 blurt) "If you don't stop that right now, there will be no going to your father's house tonight!" You accompany this yelling assertion with a very stern look, hoping against hope that your child stops! You are so tired of her acting-up today, and it seems to be escalating the closer visitation time gets. You know your child is looking forward to seeing her dad, so just maybe, threatening her not going will get her attention. Something has to work. Nothing else has.

But it continues…

(#2 blurt) "Wait till your father hears about this!" That's it. You've had enough. Your patience expired a long time ago. You're now furious at your child's continual acting-up, and it's time your ex gets a taste of what real life with your child is all about. He won't put up with it, and your child knows it. Now your child knows that you mean business.

♥ *When it comes to disciplining your child, focus on your child, not methods that focus on your divorce.*

The *Pro ♥ Child* Way

Using your child's father as a threat or denying visitation rank high on the "top-ten things not to say when divorced." Parenting after divorce isn't rocket-science, but it does require an extra step of consideration. Consider this: anytime you invoke the "Dad = threat" phrase, your child will suffer.

(#1 blurt) "No going to your father's house!" Indeed, there are many reasons why you shouldn't threaten Dad, but for these purposes, the main reason is this: you're letting your child's behavior control the visitation schedule. Reach back to Section 1 and recite the rule: ***never change the visitation schedule.*** Likewise, never should your child's moods or actions cause a change in the visitation schedule. Going to Dad's house is not a reward for good behavior. Going to Dad's house is not revoked for bad behavior. Visitation happens, regardless. If you really want ill behavior to explode, just deny visitation once. Once is all the lesson your child needs to start acting-up on visitation days. It makes no difference if she actually enjoys her visits with Dad. Her newfound control will be wielded by her simply for control sake.

Now, this isn't to say that your child can commit a dastardly crime and leave unpunished, just because visitation is starting in a moment. Your ex's car shouldn't be your child's getaway car. The best way to curtail negative behavior is to inflict immediate consequences. Even in the shortest spaces of time, you can interrupt your child's behavior. As you force your child to sit while she's "waiting for Dad" instead of her usual running around, you can assure her that her behavior was not appreciated.

(#2 blurt) Well, the first problem that comes to mind when you say "wait till your father hears about this" is how your child is going to respond. It may affect her attitude, but it probably won't affect her behavior at all. Why should it? When you witnessed her inappropriate behavior, you didn't do anything — except threaten with her dad. When you do tell her dad, he'll probably do the same thing that you did: nothing. Your child may as well continue on in destruction while her parents continue on in their threats.

The second, more insidious effect is that you are portraying your ex in a negative light. All of a sudden the focus is no longer on your child's negative behavior, but rather on your feelings towards your ex. You are directly implying that your ex is meaner, more unreasonable, and downright horrible. Encourage your child to have a positive relationship with her dad. Don't suggest that your child should fear him. Perhaps your personal opinion of your ex isn't too positive, but sharing it with your child serves no benefit to her. Your role as a parent is to portray your child's father in the best light. As the saying goes, if you have nothing nice to say, then say nothing at all. Get back to the business at hand: immediately respond to your child's behavior.

"There will be no going to your father's house tonight" and "wait till your father hears about this" are two phrases that should be immediately removed from your discipline-after-divorce arsenal. When it comes to disciplining your child, focus on your child, not methods that focus on your divorce.

Divorced Situation 45

DISCIPLINE: Discuss Incidences with Your Ex

There is a wrong reason and a right reason for telling your ex about your child's discipline incidences. The wrong reason is focused on you and your ex. The right reason is focused on your child. Discuss discipline incidences with your ex, so that your child is raised in love, concern, consistency, and structure. Choose to discuss your child's behavior issues in the Pro♥Child Way.

The Old Way

The evidence is clear: your child, a crayon, and doodles all over the wall. As you are screaming at your child, you reach for the phone and dial your ex. Instead of "Hello," you shriek, "Do you know what your child just did? That child of yours…" spewing out the tale. You're tired of your child's acting up, and you're tired of your ex not doing a thing about it.

You are always the one that has to deal with your child's discipline. You deal with her messy room. You deal with her food issues. You deal with her acting up at school. You deal with her attitude. It is you and always you. You are tired, stressed, and fed-up. It's time for your ex to take some responsibility. This time, your ex will have to deal with it because now it's his problem, not yours. He is always so quick to judge you; now you get to judge his response, now you'll really get to show him how tiring it all can be.

You hand the phone over to your child and wait to see what happens. This time your ex will have to say something. This time, he'll see what you have to put up with.

♥ *The point of communicating is simply to share information so that both parents are aware of and better equipped to handle discipline issues.*

The *Pro ♥ Child* Way

But, what about your child? What does your child need? What is best for your child? This isn't about you being tired and stressed. This isn't about your issues with your ex. This isn't about your ex. This is your child's issue. Your only role as a parent is to handle it. Shrieking at your ex and bemoaning your troubles isn't handling it. All that commotion has nothing to do with your child.

When you call your ex in front of your child, you are not discussing your child's discipline issues with your ex – you are being a tattletale. A tattletale's only purpose is to look like the hero while someone else gets into trouble. Children are tattletales and then they mature. My advice to you: grow up.

The point of communicating with your ex isn't for you to be the sympathetic victim or for your child to get into trouble. The point of communicating is simply to share information so that both parents are aware of and better equipped to handle discipline issues.

Talk to your ex privately. While your child should be aware that you and her dad share information relating to her, she shouldn't directly hear your conversation. Tell your ex – don't shriek, scream, insinuate, or blame. This isn't about him looking bad and you looking good. This also isn't about trying to get your child into more trouble. Double punishment isn't the goal. The point is to relay what happened. Who knows, maybe your ex has experienced the same problem and will have some good advice. This *is* possible. Maybe you can give your ex a heads-up with a potential recurring situation. Or, maybe you're ex will be totally nonchalant about the whole thing. In any case, your job is well done: you handled your child's discipline issue, and you communicated it with your ex.

The point of this communication is to provide the best basis for parenting. The more information you have, the better parent you'll be. The more information that your ex has, the better parent he'll be. By sharing the discipline issues and previous responses, both parents can better identify larger behavioral problems. It will also help to keep smaller infractions in perspective.

After the incident is communicated, casually relay to your child the fact that her dad is aware of the issue. Don't tell your child in a threatening or intimidating way. A simple statement will suffice. "When I talked to Dad today, I told him about your drawing on the walls. I told him that we then cleaned it up together. That was hard work, wasn't it?" You don't need to be dramatic. Your child will get the subtle message: she has two parents that talk.

When parenting, it's nice to have backup – especially when it comes to your child's discipline. Share information with your ex, and listen when your ex shares with you. Keep the attention and the process focused on your child.

Divorced Situation 46

DISCIPLINE: Different Places, Different Disciplines

When you were married, chances are, one parent took the lead on matters of discipline. Perhaps one parent was just naturally better at handling tough parenting situations while the other parent had a knack for tuning it out. Maybe your ex's method of discipline wasn't the approach that you preferred he would have taken. Before and after the divorce, your child has two parents: two parents who each have their own discipline styles. Focus on disciplining your child as the parent you are, not as the divorced ex that you've become.

The Old Way

Your child just came home from her time with your ex and she is in tears. As the "good" parent, you're there to dissect every sentence that she sobs. You piece together the story. You hear her bemoan: "Dad did…," and you zoom into hear what the evil ex did. You hear: "He doesn't understand me," and you shake your head in disgust thinking back to all the times your ex didn't understand your feelings. You hear: "It's not fair," and you burst forth: "Oh baby! I'm sooo sorry. I know your father just doesn't understand anything. He never gets it right. He is always overreacting…."

Your child just baited you with the "evil-ex" ploy. You took the bait, and you are enjoying the invitation to spew how horrible your ex really is. What instigated your ex's response? Who cares! Here is the formula that matters: crying child = evil ex. Clearly, it is your ex's fault that your child is devastated. How dare he. Your poor, poor child. Your child is perfect. Your ex clearly overreacted, and you're more than happy to jump aboard the boo-hoo train and commiserate with your child. Your energies are poured into consoling your child and formulating your response. You don't respond to your child about her instigating actions, but you sure do respond to your child about her father's reaction.

Super Mom to the rescue! Here is yet another chance for you to rescue your child from the grips of the evil-ex, proving how you're the hero and her father is the villain. As the sun goes down, your cape waves victoriously in the winds of righteousness. The evil ex is no match for you. Mom has saved the day. You've made sure that he'll think twice about making your daughter cry.

♡ *Whether you agree or not with your ex's approach, you have no control over his parenting style. No matter what your opinion, stay focused on your child and not on your ex.*

The *Pro ♥ Child* Way

Your child just came home from her time with her dad and she is in tears. As a good mom, you're there to hear what happened. Through her sobs you gather that her dad reacted to something she did. You hear: "Dad did…," and you wonder what prompted him to discipline her. You hear: "He doesn't understand me," and you prod her to tell you the whole story. You hear: "It's not fair," and you quietly say, "Honey, tell me what happened."

As the story unwinds, your child ices over her infraction, but goes into detail about how her dad completely overreacted. He yelled. He screamed. He embarrassed her in front of her friends. He made her leave her friend's house early, plus he took away her phone privileges for the rest of the night. During a dramatic pause in her story, you say, "Ummmm, what exactly is it that you did?" Instead of focusing on your ex and his reaction, you stay focused on your child and the infraction. Did he indeed overreact? Is your child justified in her tearful response? Does your child need to be rescued? Or, does your child need to hear you support her dad's decision to discipline his way?

For fun, let's think of possible infractions. Let's say that your 14-year-old daughter was caught smoking at her friend's house. Would you have reacted sternly? Ah, yeah. It's fair to assume that you would have **reacted.** You would have yelled and screamed in front of her friends. You would have marched her into the car to go home early, and it's for sure that she wasn't going to be allowed to jump on the phone and compare tales with her friends. All in all, you would have reacted in a similar manner as your ex. He did what you would have done. To score his reaction, you would have to give it a thumbs-up. Your child is now crying, and you feel for her. But her dad's discipline is what it is. And discipline doesn't usually end with an immediately joyous child.

But what if the infraction wasn't smoking, what if it was less black and white? What if during your child's sleepover at her friend's house, she called her dad because while fooling around she mussed-up her pajamas? When he got to the friend's house, instead of dropping off her new pajamas, he went ballistic, screaming about how irresponsible she was. In front of her friends, he went nuts and made her get into the car and go home. She was devastated and couldn't even call her friends for comfort. Would you have reacted this sternly? No, and hearing this puts a knot in your stomach. You can't believe how your ex overreacted. You absolutely would not have reacted in a similar manner as your ex. He did not do what you would have done. To score his reaction, you would give it a thumbs-down. Your child is now crying, and you feel for her. But her dad's reaction is what it is. You can't control him or his reactions. You can only teach your child to weather the storm.

In both cases, your ex disciplined his child. Whether you agree or not with your ex's approach, you have no control over his parenting style. No matter what your opinion, stay focused on your child and not on your ex. This isn't a time to further punish her bad behavior, nor is it a time to ignore her behavior and only concentrate on bashing your ex's response. This is your opportunity to ask her questions, listen to how she feels, and ask her how she would do things differently if given the chance. This is her time to grow and learn. This is not your time to prove a point. In the case of an overreacting ex, your job is to teach your child to see the best in him by guiding her through steps of understanding and coping. You may need to take a few deep breaths to make it through, but your child's relationship with her dad is worth it. So long as his reactions aren't cause for a "Protection from Abuse Order," your child will continue to be with him. Teach her how to do that. With your guidance, your child can still gain and learn from the experience.

While different places may mean different disciplines for your child, you can choose consistency within your own home. You can control how you handle discipline issues with your child at home; and when she is away, you can control how you guide her through her experiences. This is what being a good parent is all about.

www.TheProChildWay.com

Ellen Kellner has experienced how powerful the Pro♥Child approach to divorce can be. Twice. Because of this mindful approach, her two daughters are blessed to have a mom and dad, plus a whole pack of extended friends and family who love them and add smiles to their lives.

Through her speaking and writing, Ellen continues to bring the message of *The Pro♥Child Way* to parents who are looking for a transformative approach to divorce parenting. A graduate of The American University, Ellen continues to study, learn, and broaden her awareness of our greater spiritual existence and how that applies to all of our relationships, including the relationship with an ex.

"In the book, **The Pro♡Child Way: Parenting with an Ex**, Ellen Kellner shares tools, techniques, and stories from her heart, to help support divorced parents to be the best they can be for the sake of their children. I have seen first hand how Ellen practices what she preaches. She is an exceptional mom, and her daughters are blessed to have her. She takes her role as a co-parent seriously and is an unbelievable role model for her daughters, as well as for all of us who are parenting with an ex."

—Joanie Winberg, Founder
National Association of Divorce for Women and Children
Lakeville, MA

'**The Pro♡Child Way** is the book every parent going through a divorce should be required to read. This book offers guidance and hope for divorcing parents who know the importance intact parenting can have on the lives of their children. It is written for parents who have a strong desire to meet the personal and emotional needs of their children during and after a divorce. Ellen Kellner's child-centered or Pro♡Child solutions to a myriad of divorce situations provide parents with the ability to better understand their child's perspective and to then act accordingly in the best interest of their child."

—Bonnie Manning, Director
Children's House of Hershey Montessori

"Ellen Kellner writes with compassion and humor ... bringing to light a much-needed perspective to parenting in divorced situations. You can't go wrong with keeping the needs of children first!"

—Kris Robino
Elementary Guidance Counselor licensed in Pennsylvania

"Nearly half of all marriages in America end in divorce. Thank you, Ellen Kellner, for giving a voice to the millions of American children affected by divorce."

—Michelle Allen, Licensed Psychologist
PhD in Human Development